# WAR REVOLUTION & JAPAN

# War
# Revolution
# & Japan

## EDITED BY
## Ian Neary

 RoutledgeCurzon
Taylor & Francis Group

LONDON AND NEW YORK

WAR REVOLUTION & JAPAN
First published 1993
By Japan Library.
Reprinted 2004
by RoutledgeCurzon,
2 Park Square, Milton Park,
Abingdon, Oxon, OX14 4RN

Transferred to Digital Printing 2004

© Japan Library 1993

ISBN 1–873410–08–5

**British Library Cataloguing in Publication Data**
A CIP catalogue record for this book
is available from the British Library

Set in Garamond Light 11 on 12 point
by Bookman, Slough, Berks

# Contents

# Preface

THESE PAPERS are selected from the History, Politics and International Relations section at the Sixth Conference of the European Association of Japanese Studies which was held in September 1991 in the Japanese-German Centre, Berlin (JGCB). This was a rewarding and enjoyable experience made possible by the hard work of the President of the EAJS, Professor Sepp Linhart and the staff of the JGCB.

The Japan Foundation supported the conference in several ways, not least by funding the visits of several key speakers from Japan, one of whom, Professor T. Kato from Hitotsubashi University, gave a paper that appears in this collection.

The trustees of the Great Britain-Sasakawa Foundation provided a generous grant which has facilitated the publication of this volume. Our publisher, Paul Norbury, provided the encouragement to deliver the manuscripts sooner rather than later.

Finally I would like to express my thanks to Dr Wolfgang Seifert of Heidelberg University for the assistance he gave me in coordinating the arrangements for this History section of the conference. I look forward to working with him again.

IAN NEARY
*July 1992*
Colchester

# Contributors

JOHN CRUMP is a Senior Lecturer in Politics at the University of York. He is the author of *Hatta Shūzō and 'Pure Anarchism' in Interwar Japan* (forthcoming from Macmillan).

OLAVI FÄLT is a Senior Researcher of the Academy of Finland and teaches in the Department of History, University of Oulu. He has written on the relationship between Finland and Japan in the period up to 1945 and on the role of the Emperor as a national symbol in the Taishō era.

KARINE MARANDJIAN is a Researcher in the history of Japan at the Institute of Oriental Studies, St Petersburg. She is at present pursuing her research at the International Research Centre for Japanese Studies in Kyoto.

JULIA MIKHAILOVA is a Researcher at the Institute of Oriental Studies, St Petersburg.

MARGARET MEHL is Yasuda Trust and Banking Fellow in Japanese Studies at the Faculty of Oriental Studies in Cambridge University. She is the author of Eine Vergangenheit für die Japanische Nation. Die Entstehung des historischen Forschungsinstituts *Tōkyō daigaku Shiryō bensanjo* (1869–1995), (Verlag Peter Lang,).

KATO TETSURO is Professor of Political Science in the Faculty of Social Studies at Hitotsubashi University, Tokyo, Japan. He is author of *Comintern no Sekaizo* (Aoki Shoten, 1991), *Soren Hōkai to Shakai-shugi* (Iwanami Shoten, 1992) and *Shakai to Kokka* (Iwanami Shoten, 1992).

ISONO FUJIKO taught family sociology at Japan Women's University and at Japan College of Social Work and is now an independent research worker on the history of family ideology.

ULRIKE WÖHR was an Assistant at the Institute of Japanology at Heidelberg University. She is currently conducting research at Waseda University for her doctoral dissertation which looks into women's magazines in the first years of the Taishō era.

BEN-AMI SHILLONY is Professor of Japanese history at the Hebrew University of Jerusalem, Israel. He is author of *Revolt in Japan* (Princeton, 1973), *Politics and Culture in Wartime Japan* (Oxford, 1981) and *Jews and the Japanese* (Tokyo, 1992).

DAVID WILLIAMS has taught Japanese government and politics at Oxford University. He is presently a contributing editorial writer for *The Japan Times* and comments regularly on Japanese and European affairs for the *Los Angeles Times*. His new book, *Thinking Nationalism: The Japanese Approach to Public Policy* will be published by Routledge in 1993.

ANTHONY WOODIWISS is a Senior Lecturer in the Department of Sociology at Essex University. He has been visiting Professor of Sociology at Dokkyo University. He contributed 'Rereading Japan: Possession, Law and Hegemony' to N. Abercrombie (ed) *Discourses of Dominance* (Unwin Hyman, 1990). He is author of *Law, Labour and Society in Japan* (Routledge, 1991).

# Introduction

IAN NEARY

REVOLUTION was still in the air in Berlin in September 1991. The previous month an attempted coup by army officers in Moscow had seemed poised to reverse the liberalisation of the Soviet Union. Its failure led to the rapid unravelling of the Soviet state, a process whose consequences are still not at all clear. What is clear and what was commonly felt, is that we had been witnessing, even participating in a series of events at least as important for Russia and the wider world as was the Meiji Ishin (the events of 1868) for Japan and world history. Our experience of contemporary changes made the discussion about Revolution and Japan seem more immediately relevant than is often the case at international academic conferences.

The EAJS conference organisers selected Berlin as the location for their 1991 sessions well before anyone suspected the extent and speed of the revolution which would sweep across Central and Eastern Europe. But, as it turned out, Berlin was the ideal location for the first international Japanese studies conference of the post-Cold War era. More scholars from Eastern Europe than ever before were able to attend the conference and were able to participate freely in the discussions for the first time. (Some, hitherto familiar, faces were missing but this fact was diplomatically not commented on.) The scholars who were able to attend brought not only the fruits of their research to inform the debate but also the experience of their own revolutions to enliven the discussion.

There were two sessions where this became dramatically obvious. In one session Dr Cherevko of the Soviet Academy of Science gave an impromptu paper on the problem of the Northern Territories. This amounted to a critical discussion of the Soviet Union's stand on the issue given by a member of the staff which briefed the Soviet diplomats. Issues were outlined and positions discussed with a frankness that would have been impossible only a few weeks earlier. Later in the conference, when Professor Katō presented his paper, he discussed the way in which the events in Poland and elsewhere were reported in the Japanese media. Several

1

members of the audience had acted as guides for Japanese reporters and television crews and they were able to explain how Japan received the reports it did. Unusually for an academic conference there was a very real feeling that what was taking place in the conference sessions was clearly linked to events on the streets and in offices elsewhere in the world.

Not all the papers presented to the History, Politics and International Relations section were relevant to our theme of War, Revolution and Japan; only those which relate to that theme appear in this collection. The historical range of the papers is broad: from discussion of the Tokugawa view of Japan's place in the world to the relevance of the 'Japanese model' for the development of Eastern Europe in the 1990s and beyond. There is no decade of the post-Restoration era that escapes the attention of our authors although each of them is writing with a specific and particular purpose.

Marandjian discusses the emergence of one of the key concepts which made the Meiji Restoration possible – the formation of Japanese nationalism in the Tokugawa era. The problem for Confucian intellectuals (and most of the Tokugawa regime's intellectuals were Confucian) was how to reconcile the antagonism between their growing pride in their own national tradition and the idea of China as the 'cultured', 'civilised' country, which suggested conversely that the rest of the world was peripheral and barbarian. She suggests that Chie Nakane's discussion of the importance of 'superior–inferior' type of relations assists our understanding of the development of Tokugawa thought in relation to China, especially following the emergence of a European, Christian threat from the late eighteenth century onwards. This shifted Japan's perception of the outside world from one which looked only at East Asia and relations between East Asian states to one which had to include Europeans. Within this new context the Europeans were cast into the role of the barbarians and the concept of 'middle kingdom' could be constructed to include both China and Japan. There remained some problems about how Japan should relate to China and Korea since there was no concept of parity of nation states but pride in belonging to the central set of states could now be justified with reference to a Confucian framework.

The idea that Japan inherited the role of 'central' or

'middle kingdom' is an important stream within the thought of Tokugawa intellectuals. As Shillony makes clear, it is also a notion that inspired many of those who were actively involved in the process of the Meiji Restoration and who implemented the reforms which were adopted thereafter. By the end of the Meiji period they had successfully reconstructed East Asia with Japan at its centre, the Ryukyu Islands and Taiwan its colonies and China its satellite, politically, economically and intellectually. Moreover, its nominal ruler, the Meiji Tennō, was the only reigning emperor in the region.

If one Japanese official interpretation of the events in the late nineteenth century followed Confucian patterns, Russian interpretations of the same set of events have followed a very different orthodoxy. Mikhailova provides us with a summary of the three main periods of Soviet Japanese studies and the interpretations of the Meiji Ishin that are central to each of them. In post-revolutionary Russia the attempts of Marxist historians to interpret the Meiji Ishin encountered the difficulty of assessing whether it could be described as a bourgeois revolution despite the fact that there was practically no evidence of a bourgeois class. At this stage Soviet studies of Japan were clearly linked to the revolutionary and political struggle in Japan even though their understanding of Japan in the 1920s was poor. After the war scholarly attention primarily concentrated on revealing the roots of capitalistic relations in the Tokugawa period. In the 1950s and 1960s while Western scholars were reconsidering the Meiji Ishin in terms of theories of 'modernisation', Soviet scholars were keen to deny any positive importance of the Japanese experience, preferring instead to emphasise the heavy price paid for rapid development by the people of Japan and others elsewhere in Asia. Only in the 1980s was a more sophisticated theory devised to place Japan into the context of various models of capitalist development. However, Mikhailova concludes, a thorough analysis of the Japanese historical data from this theoretical perspective remains incomplete and thus we still await an original, Russian contribution to the analysis of the Meiji Ishin.

The Japanese ruling class were as aware as the CPSU leaders of the power of history as legitimator of political practice and reforms. Margaret Mehl's contribution to this set of essays describes the fluctuations in the fortunes of

3

what was to become the Historiographical Institute (*Tōkyō Daigaku Shiryō Hensanjo*). Her account illustrates the way in which policy towards the compilation of an official history varied in line with the political problems facing the Meiji government. For example, in 1873, faced by a growing challenge from the People's Rights Movement, the Council of State was reorganised and an announcement was made promising the gradual establishment of constitutional government, at the same time a new 'Office of Historiography' (*shū'shikyoku*) was created. Later in the Meiji period it was the Meiji Ishin itself which would become the object of historical interpretation. By this time it was no longer necessary to justify the actions of officials in reference to Japan's ancient history; the Meiji Ishin had created a set of new traditions which had the power to serve the present.

By the end of the Meiji period there was the first glimmer of the emergence of a dissenting intellectual tradition which resisted some of the official claims being made about Japan, its place in the world and the role of the individual within Japanese society. Two essays in this collection are detailed descriptions of groups which offered an alternative view of existing Japan and different visions of its future. Ulrike Wöhr offers an account of the development of the Shinshin Fujinkai (True New Woman's Society). This was a contemporary of, though much less well known than, the Seitōsha (Blue Stocking Society).

Wöhr gives us a rounded view of the Shinshin Fujinkai by providing brief biographies of its three founders, describing the book they wrote as co-authors and discussing the contents of the earliest editions of the journal they produced. Whilst wanting to demonstrate that there was more to the early phase of the Japan's women's movement than the Seitōsha she refers frequently to it as a useful basis for comparison. So, for example, compared to the young ladies of the Seitōsha, the key figures of the Shinshin Fujinkai were both wives and mothers, but they seem to have been more determined to organise themselves without the support of men. In the first volume of the journal they pride themselves on publishing it 'without depending on any direct help from men'. They were critical of the way women were taught to view themselves by society and proposed ways in which a 'New Woman' might emerge.

However, they had little time for socialism or anarchism and seem to have been ideologically influenced chiefly by religious notions current at the time. There was also an attempt to publicise and explain what was happening in the women's movement in Europe and America. Our understanding of Taishō Democracy is enriched by knowledge of these less well known movements.

Anarchism was much more powerful within the mass movements of the 1920s than most accounts allow, whether they be written in Japanese or English. As John Crump has argued elsewhere, anarchist trade unions continued to attract a significant body of support until the general collapse of trade unions in the face of increasingly intense state repression in the 1930s (see 'The Japanese Pure Anarchists and the Theory of Anarchist Communism' in *Western Interactions with Japan*; ed. P. Lowe and H. Moeshart, Japan Library, 1991, pp. 33–49). Not only did they remain numerically strong but key elements within the anarchist movement demonstrated an intellectual vitality which developed theoretical notions beyond the level found in Europe. One such theoretician was Hatta Shūzō (1886–1934) the principal theoretician of the 'pure anarchists'. In the essay included in this compilation John Crump argues that there is a great deal in common between 'pure anarchist' thought and that of the Green movement in that they sought to achieve a society '. . . immeasurably Greener than the path towards industrialisation, urbanisation, militarism and imperialism that Japanese capitalism actually took'. Although conceding that the vocabulary used was quite different, he concludes 'these "pure anarchists" can be regarded as one movement among probably many which were Green even before the term was even coined.'

The Emperor was central to the historical and cultural tradition invented by the Meiji oligarchs to legitimate their regime to enable them to dismiss liberal and more radical critics as foreign to the essence of the Japanese way of life. The status of the Emperor within the political structure and his role within the cultural tradition becomes crucial during the war years of the 1930s and 1940s. Olavi Fält's paper examines the way the activities of the Emperor were recorded in two English language newspapers, the *Nippon Times* and *Osaka Mainichi/Tōkyō Nichi Nichi*, both of which continued to be published until the end of the war. The newspapers, although mildly critical of the aspirations to political hegemony entertained in military circles, were quite uncritical of the description of events connected with the mythical emergence of Japan and its first Emperor, Jimmu. Until 1938 both newspapers tried to defend constitutional government from a liberal, democratic position, but thereafter reference to the Emperor was made with a view to strengthening the nation's fighting spirit. Later, as the prospect of defeat loomed, so still more energy was devoted to propagating the traditional view of the founding of the imperial dynasty. By the spring of 1945 these newspapers were clearly expressing the anxiety that the continuity of Imperial rule was under threat.

The abolition of the Emperor system and even his trial as a war criminal were advocated by some of the Allied Powers. Although committed to a programme of democratisation, the American army of occupation in the person of General MacArthur refused to proceed with such a revolutionary proposal. Isono Fujiko in her reflections on the post-surrender democratisation of Japan suggests that in the area of social structure and popular mentality the changes which took place amounted to much less than a thorough democratisation. Using examples from the change (or lack of it) in the family system, the lack of social equality within the factory and the absence of a genuine respect for human rights in Japan, Isono concludes that 'the real transformation of Japanese subjects into modern citizens . . . a revolution of mentality, seems to be still far away'.

Anthony Woodiwiss pursues a similar theme in his study examining the (re)interpretation of labour law in Japan. His argument echoes that of Isono in maintaining that despite the apparently revolutionary Trade Union Act of 1946, there has been a persistence of social-structured continuities between pre- and post-war Japan which has led to a partial reversal of this revolution. Through an examination of the statutes of the later 1940s and the case law which has emerged over the last 50 years, he shows how the sociological–ideological foundation which he (among others) calls *kigyōism* has continued the hostility of the pre-war Tennōsei towards fully autonomous and assertive trade unions. Moreover the trend has been towards an increasingly restrictive interpretation of the rights of employees and their union representatives. Most worrying of all he suggests that the unions themselves have colluded in this process.

Katō Tetsuro was the invited speaker at the conference and his attendance was made possible by support from the

Japan Foundation. As the key speaker in our sessions he was allowed twice as long as the others to develop his ideas and, as presented here, the paper is substantially longer than any of the others in the compilation. His theme was how the 1989 Eastern European Revolutions were perceived in Japan and in developing it he considers more aspects than it is possible to summarise here. His basic approach is that although Japanese people are aware of world news soon after it occurs, they rarely perceive it as likely to have an immediate impact on their lives.

The first third of the paper is a discussion of how 'revolution' is conceived of by different sections of the Japanese population. In this he refers back to ideas that are first touched on by authors of the papers earlier in this volume. From this he proceeds to describe the different impacts that the news from Europe had on the Diet parties from the LDP through to the JCP. He also sketches out the first responses of the groups that exist behind, or to one side of, the Diet parties: the leftist intellectual community, Japan's business leaders and finally the Japanese people as a whole. In relation to this latter group he finds them 'economy centred' at least compared to their US equivalents and overwhelmingly passive towards events both at home and abroad. Such passivity can be regarded as one result of the dubious success of Japanese management practices of the kind discussed by Woodiwiss. However, Katō is undismayed by this. Prior to 1989 the peoples of Eastern Europe seemed passive, concerned only with their daily lives but very rapidly their attitudes changed from superficial disagreement to great discontent. There is a possibility, he suggests, that at a time when neither politicians nor bureaucrats display a national vision, the Japanese people may be stimulated by the 1989 Eastern European revolutions to promoting a series of (revolutionary?) changes in Japan.

The 'Learning from Japan' boom swept Western Europe and North America in the 1980s and, although it has developed more sophisticated variants, it continues to be a consistent theme in popular writing about Japan. Katō mentions in his essay the way visitors from the former Soviet Union and East Europe have recently visited Japan to discover the secrets of the 'Japanese model' or 'Japanese management'. David Williams in the final paper in this compilation suggests that one can see in Japan 'a subtle and complex design for fostering civil society . . . that is capable of clear statement'. In contrast to the free market model which had been proposed as the solution to the East European problems, the experience of Japan suggests a 'third way' in which 'political ends are given preference over economic interest'. On the one hand Japan provides a practical model of the creation of a civil society based on pragmatic thought and experiment. On the other he suggests that it is the political philosophy of Hegel which can provide the theoretical basis for understanding this process. The Anglo-American free market tradition concentrates its attention on the profit-maximising individual whereas the Hegelian tradition insists that society is more than just a collection of individuals: it also includes both the family and the state.

Within this latter frame of reference the nation and the nation state are perceived as playing an important political role. This is in stark contrast to the view of the free market right (and socialist left) who have typically regarded the nation state as little more than a convenient political fiction. No nineteenth- or twentieth-century European nationalist would accept this nor would the state builders of post-war East Asia. Nationalisms seem to be the most powerful forces in Eastern Europe. Williams argues that the monetarist prescriptions for reform which ignore this are inappropriate. Rather than Western Europe or North America it is to the recent political and economic experience of East Asia that the nation builders of the post-communist states should look, especially to Japan. In Japan '. . . the Meiji reformers built their plans around the Japanese realities inherited from the Tokugawa, just as the future Central and Eastern Europe must be built on what history and regional values have made those Europeans'.

* * *

Until a few years ago it seemed that the study of revolution was the proper domain of historians. The world appeared stable and few predicted any great change in its geographical or political dimensions. In the early 1990s it now appears that the apparent stability was more like a log jam; it only required relatively small changes to permit tumultuous change (revolutions?) whose consequences for good and ill are still unclear. Periods of rapid change are not new. The thirty years 1840–70 saw revolution in many areas of the world as did the ten years after the end of the Great War and the five years following the Second World War. The destructive phase of the 1989 East European revolutions now seems over but it is unclear what can be constructed amid the ruins of the state socialist systems. It will be a prolonged process as the scale of economic and political reconstruction is huge. It seems also likely to be painful as regional and religious rivalries, suppressed for 50 years or more, re-emerge. Only an optimist would suggest that this will end with the triumphant adoption of liberal democratic principles. The ends of history as perceived by North Americans are not seen in the same way by Central Europeans or East Asians.

This volume marks a tentative step to explain how the Japanese fit into this picture. In the 130 or so years that are covered by these essays we see the Japanese moving from a preoccupation with their place in the world in which the key referent was China, the Central Kingdom. Following a revolution in the form of the Meiji Ishin, reforms were initiated which enabled Japan to replace China as the central power in East Asia by the start of the twentieth century. Shrugging off demands that Japan engage in further reform, the government used the traditions, images and machinery of state created within the Meiji constitutional structure to unite the nation behind aggressive policies in Asia that brought it into conflict with the ailing, but still proud, imperialist nations of Britain, France and Holland and, more importantly, the United States. Following defeat, the US occupiers insisted the Japanese carry out reform based on the American model at the same time as reforms based on the Soviet model were being imposed in Eastern Europe.

At the two extremes of the Eurasian continent nations struggled to make work systems of government of alien origin. From the perspective of the early 1990s the revolution imposed on Japan appears to have been more benign in its effects than those imposed on Eastern Europe. It was the rigidity of the systems in Eastern Europe that required them to be passively accepted or actively rejected. In contrast, the flexibility of the regime in Japan has allowed the single-party-dominant state to remain in power with no prospect on the horizon that it will be replaced by another party or rejected in a show of 'people's power' of an East European type. Will the Japanese state be able to retain this flexibility?

# 1

# Some aspects of the Tokugawa outer world view

KARINE MARANDJIAN

IT IS GENERALLY accepted that the Tokugawa epoch was a period of the formation of Japanese nationalism, the development of self-consciousness and the growth of national pride. One of the major problems of the time was that of Japan's self-image – the evolution of Japan's role in the world order, the estimation of the character of the Chinese civilisation and Japan's attitude to the idea of China's centrality.

The process of the reconsideration of China's role took on various forms. On the official government level the Bakufu, wishing to confirm its growing autonomous structure of legitimacy, declared an independence from the so-called 'Chinese world order', the content of which in a simplified form can be brought to the division of the world into the civilised centre (China) and uncivilised periphery and the idea of the transformative power of the Chinese Emperor, the mediator between heaven and man, responsible for maintaining order in the world. Japan not only rejected the sinocentric order dominant in East Asia, but established an alternative, Japan-centred order of international relations. By rejecting direct government-to-government relations with China, the Bakufu relegated China to the lowest 'barbarian' level of international hierarchy. This process was completed in the second decade of the eighteenth century. (See R.P. Toby, *State and Diplomacy in Early Modern Japan. Asia in the development of the Tokugawa Bakufu*. Princeton, 1984, p. 197.)

On the non-government, intellectual level this problem was formulated and understood as the problem of the validity of the Chinese scheme 'The Middle Kingdom – barbarians' and of the use of the traditional terms 'Middle Kingdom' (*chūgoku*) and 'barbarians' in general.

For Tokugawa Confucians it was a very delicate question

10

creating a certain psychological unease because it brought their feelings towards China as a larger older civilisation to which Japan owed an immense cultural debt and of the immutably sinocentric characteristics of Confucianism into conflict with their national feelings towards their own country. As Kate W. Nakai puts it, 'the early Tokugawa Confucians found themselves walking a tightrope' (K.W. Nakai 'The naturalisation of Confucianism in Tokugawa Japan: the problem of sinocentrism', in *Harvard Journal of Asiatic Studies*, Vol. 40, N 1, 1980, p. 159). Naturally, no Tokugawa Confucian could easily accept the identification of their country with 'barbarian' status. This was partly due to the fact that in reality their ideal-China was conquered by an alien 'barbarian' dynasty and partly due to the Japanese self-perception, based on the mythology of imperial divinity, which 'made the acknowledgment of any supervening authority extremely difficult' (R.P. Toby, *op.cit.*, p. 172). Discussion of the 'Middle kingdom–barbarians' scheme gave rise to various opinions and interpretations. Some scholars stressed the idea of the centrality of Japan, identifying it with the term *chugoku*; others, upholding the normative character of the Chinese scheme, tried to substantiate the uniqueness of Japanese civilisation. There is no need to trace in detail different approaches to the solution of the problem; they have already been studied by a number of researchers.

As was mentioned, Tokugawa scholars discussing the applicability of the *ka-i* scheme were confronted with a painful dilemma: within the framework of Confucian values they could not doubt the validity of the *ka-i* division, but within the framework of their national self-perception they could not accept it. They had to elaborate very skilful explanations that would disguise their ambivalent attitude and allow them to create a delicate balance paving the way for an admissible solution. From this standpoint the approach of Sato Naokata, one of the most famous disciples of Yamazaki Ansai, deserves special attention as an original way out of this contradiction.

Sato Naokata (1650–1719) is known as an ardent adherent of Chu Hsi's Confucianism, dismissed from the Kimon school for his sharp disagreement with Yamazaki Ansai's Shinto studies. Traditional opinion of Naokata criticises him for 'his praising China as the central civilisation and insulting his own country'. For example Sajja A. Prasad considers him to be 'averse and antagonistic to all theories of Japan, Japan's Emperor, Japan's Way . . .' and 'absolutist on the Middle country (i.e. China) that was organising and recurrently moralising the world' (Sajja A. Prasad, *Studies in sinological sex, religion, racism and nationalism*, Vol. 1. 'The Patriotism thesis and argument in Tokugawa Japan including some Shinto strictures on Buddhist treason and China sinologist sinolatry', part 1, 1975, pp. 37–9). This rather widespread appraisal of Sato Naokata's position is unconvincing and can be disputed.

This analysis of his ideas is made on the basis of the treatise entitled 'Collected treatises on the [concept] of Middle Kingdom' (*Chūgoku ronshū*) and published in the series *Japanese thought* (*Nihon shisō taikei*), Vol. 31, 'The school of Yamazaki Ansai' (*Yamazaki Ansai gakuha*). It was written as a polemical response to Asami Keisai (1652–1712), another prominent pupil of Yamazaki Ansai. Naokata's opponent, Asami Keisai, upheld the opinion that it was inadmissible to apply the *ka-i* terms to the relations between China and Japan. He declared it 'humiliating' to call his native country 'barbarian' and believed that the scheme created by the Sages was the extreme expression of their great morality understood by him as an appropriate respectful attitude towards their own country (in his words 'everyone should treat his country as his country, his parents as his parents, this is the Great Duty of Heaven and Earth'). Sato Naokata while recognising the rightfulness of the division of the Middle Kingdom (i.e. China) and barbarians asserted that to call our country 'barbarian' meant to 'emphasise a narrow-minded theory'. He also rejected the opposite extreme when Japan was identified with the Middle Kingdom. According to him the idea of Japan's superiority over China and India appeared because of 'insufficient knowledge of the Confucian scholars'. To accept this idea is to 'go against the root' (i.e. the theory promulgated by the Sages). For Naokata the origin of the scheme has predetermined its immutability and rightfulness and he could not have doubted its validity. In this case what did he mean by saying: if we consider China the centre and divide the world on behalf of China, why is it not possible to do so in behalf of Japan and Korea? Then India, Southern barbarians too must be called the Middle Kingdoms (Sato Naokata, '*Chūgoku ronshū*', in *Nihon shisō taikei*, Vol. 31, p. 423). At first sight in this fragment Sato Naokata seems to underline the relative character of the scheme, that could have been applied from different standpoints. But as Naokata observes, if we apply the scheme to different 'central' points, we would narrow the meaning of the term *chūgoku*.

I think in this passage the scholar intended to prove his reasons for withdrawing the scheme from the ethical sphere. As he says, the Middle Kingdom exists irrespectively of whether the Way is fulfilled and manifested or not. Even barbarians can obtain the Sagehood and excellent virtue (*seiken*) (Sato Naokata, *op.cit.*, p. 420). Consequently the ethical factor in his theory does not perform the function of a criterion for distinguishing the 'civilised' centre and 'uncivilised' periphery. Strictly speaking he stops dividing the world into two 'civilised' and 'uncivilised' zones. He wrote 'If we estimate the centre and barbarian lands from the standpoint of the flourishing or degradation of the Way or the Virtue, then we can say that now China is a Middle Kingdom, Korea – is a Middle Kingdom, even the neighbouring lands can change' (Sato Naokata, *op.cit.*, p. 421).

The rejection of the ethical criterion is especially evident in his discourse upon the nature of the barbarians. 'However unrighteous the man is, in fact he is not called a dog or a horse. However bad a man is, the man is a man, and a dog is a dog. The monkey is clever, nevertheless you would not say that it is like a man, even a stupid one. The parrot can speak, but it is not distinguished from other birds. To treat someone as a beast only because he contradicts the Duty is to complain of Virtue' (Sato Naokata, *op.cit.*, p. 422). It is clear from this paragraph that Naokata refutes Chu Hsi's thesis that a barbarian holds an intermediate position between human beings and animals, i.e. is not an ethical man. Thus he denies the ethical framework of the *ka-i* scheme, which constituted the essence of the traditional Confucian view on the division of the world. Naokata asserts: 'The [term] Middle Kingdom from ancient time was established in accordance with the form of the land (*chikei*). Certainly though in the Middle Kingdom the Way is manifested, the customs are good and in the barbarian [lands] they are evil, originally the establishment of the [division] between Middle Kingdom and barbarians was in conformity with the form of the land and not in conformity with the goodness or badness of customs' (Sato Naokata, *op.cit.*, p. 424).

According to him, the centre is China; its 'centrality' is due not to its moral superiority, but to the natural shape of the land. This 'geographical' approach was not a new one; in the traditional view space was considered to consist of ethically unequal parts, which is why the linking of the *ka-i* terms with the peculiarities of the 'form of the land' was outwardly quite in accord with the traditional world outlook. Nevertheless it seems doubtful that Sato Naokata, who was rejecting the ethical dimension of the *ka-i* problem, which was the kernel of the traditional approach to the world, can be designated as a proponent of a classical sinocentric view. Maybe it would be more correct to suggest that, as a Confucian thinker, he tried to substantiate the validity of the scheme, while practically revising its content, though of course, as we will see later, it was not a complete break with the traditional world view. This revision (i.e. the denial of the ethical criterion) can be explained by Naokata's aspiration to smooth the antagonism between the 'civilised' China (according to Chinese world order) and 'uncivilised' Japan and to advocate the national prestige of his native country.

Analysing the interpretation of Naokata we do not intend to assert that the removal of the scheme from the ethical framework represented the main tendency in the debates on this theme, the ideas of Sato Naokata were rather an exception to the rule. Suffice it to recall the words of Hayashi Gaho, the son of the famous Hayashi Razan, concerning Tokugawa Ieyasu: 'When the Great Divine Prince who illuminates the East unified the country . . . the barbarians were all civilised by his virtue . . .' (cited from R.P. Toby, *op.cit.*, p. 205), demonstrating the operative character of what is called the Chinese world order, applied to another 'central' point.

Despite all the distinctions between the points of view of Tokugawa Confucians their perception of the world was based on the same model – on the dichotomy between the centre and periphery (Middle Kingdom–barbarians). Convincing evidence of the operativeness of this model can be provided by the Tokugawa world maps. According to the classification of Professor Shintaro Ayusawa, there existed five types of Tokugawa world maps: objective (based on foreign originals); maps representing Buddhist cosmology (India = the Heart of the world); Chinese (China as the centre); legendary maps and world maps in which Japan (specifically Kyoto) is the centre of the world. These Japan-centred maps, as Professor Ayusawa has observed, were a reaction against Chinese and Buddhist concepts (from Hugh Cortazzi, *Isles of Gold. Antique Maps of Japan*, New York–Tokyo, 1983, p. 38). Except for the copies of European maps, all Japanese-made maps reproduced the same model – dichotomy of centre and periphery, where to the centre was assigned the function of organising the whole world. It is interesting to note the connection between the Chinese maps and the 'geographical' approach of Sato Naokata, reflecting the ideological character of traditional geography and proving that, despite Naokata's revision of the *ka-i* scheme, he still stayed within the framework of the traditional view of the external world.

The traditional Japanese outer world view (irrespective of the question of which of the three countries – India, China or Japan – was thought to be the central point) was built on the basis of one and the same structural principle, when the relations between the objects presuppose the establishment of the 'superior–inferior' type of connection. This type of tie corresponds to the 'vertical' tie that Professor Nakane Chie distinguishes as one of the most characteristic features of Japanese social organisation and Japanese culture in general (Chie Nakane, *Japanese society*, 1973, p. 146). This correspondence supplies a reason for applying Nakane's concept to the sphere of international relations, when the relations between the centre and periphery are regarded as the relations between large groups, comprising one or more countries.

First of all, let us repeat the main points of Nakane's concept. The core of the vertical structural principle is to be found in the basic social relationship between two individuals, that can be divided according to the way in which ties are organized into two categories: vertical and horizontal. Vertical systems link objects of different qualities, horizontal – of the same quality. The vertical tie functions in forming the cluster within which the upper–lower hierarchical order becomes more pronounced. Whatever variations may be found in individual cases groups in Japan are formed by the multiplication of a vertical relation. The vertical tie does not allow two or more individuals to be equal or more than one to lead.

Now let us try to analyse the type of the connection that lies at the basis of the dichotomy 'centre/Middle Kingdom –

periphery/barbarians', bearing in mind that the vertical tie links the objects of different qualities and presupposes a certain degree of hierarchy. The 'centre/Middle Kingdom' and 'periphery/barbarians' are regarded as opposite categories: the centre is civilised and the periphery is uncivilised. Their comparison is actual only in the frames of 'civilised/uncivilised' dichotomy. It gives us reason to say that the tie between centre and periphery is established between objects of different qualities. That is why it is quite natural that 'barbarians' are related to the category of 'beasts', as opposed to 'ethical human beings'.

In the 'centre–periphery' dichotomy the centre has the function of regulating the periphery, playing the dominant, leading role. So we can assume that this relation is a relation of the hierarchical type. What follows then from the identification of the vertical tie that links the social groups in Japanese society with the tie that links the 'centre' and the 'periphery'?

In a society of vertical structural principles as Nakane has noted, the equal balance of powers between peers, or collaboration between two equally competing groups is almost non-existent, 'stability always resides in imbalance between powers when one dominates the others' (Nakane Chie, *op.cit.*, p. 55). The same characteristic can be given to the system of international relations, when the world was seen in the light of the centre/Middle Kingdom and periphery/barbarians. The hierarchy that framed their relationship was the factor that made it impossible for Tokugawa Confucians to formulate the idea of parity of different parts of the world (or different countries), one of which had to dominate the other.

To illustrate this thesis let us provide one example. Confucian scholar Kumazawa Banzan (1619–1691) asserted in his *Miwa monogatari*: 'China, Japan, Korea and the Ryukyu Islands are of one kind; their manners and customs are the same – covering for the head, dress with sleeves, understanding of Chinese characters, knowledge of the Principles of Heaven' (cited from S.A. Prasad, *op.cit.*, p. 19). This passage seems to declare a certain parity of the countries that are attributed to the same category ('are of one kind'). But China, Korea, Japan and Ryukyu Islands are united only to be opposed to India, that is 'a kind apart', 'exceedingly benighted country', 'the acme of cruelty' (*ibid.*, p. 20). So the parity turns out to be the seeming parity necessary only for the confrontation with inferior India. Here the opposition 'superior–inferior' is quite evident. But the countries included in the 'superior' group also can be structured according to the dichotomy 'centre–periphery', when China is understood as the 'centre' and Japan as 'barbarian'.

A similar 'parity' passage can be found in Sato Naokata's writings, refuting the thesis that Japan, being a 'country of gods' (*shinkoku*), is superior to other countries, he poses a rhetorical question: 'What countries are China, India, Southern barbarians? . . . As if other countries do not have what is called the gods of the country of gods' (Sato Naokata, *op.cit.*, p. 424). As we have already mentioned, for Naokata the centre of the world was associated with China, the comparison of different countries on the basis of the same quality (existence of gods) does not mean that in his perception they were considered as peers. Naokata only underlines one feature which is characteristic to all these countries, i.e. he underlines certain similarities uniting them. Certainly, the idea of similarity can be regarded as a postulate that can further give rise to the acknowledgement of the equality of countries. But the debates concerning the outer world view were held in the context of traditional Confucian culture. The realisation that 'there is nowhere that is not under Heaven, that is not upborne by Earth' was inherent in this tradition from ancient times. Expressions like the above-mentioned one can be seen in abundance in Confucian (and other) texts. Yet we must assume that in the Tokugawa period the tendency to mark out certain similarity between China, Japan, India, Korea, Philippines, Indonesia, Annam (usually only these countries are compared with each other) becomes more pronounced. It seems reasonable to suggest that this tendency intensified due to acquaintance with the West, when the sense of danger coming from Europe, the 'Christian' threat, reinforced the consciousness of Japan's belonging to what we call Asian civilisation, in contrast to the countries of Christendom. Then the assertion of Fujiwara Seika that, 'as long as there is Principle', Japan, Annam, Korea and China are alike in being covered by the same heaven and upborn by the same earth, sounds as the declaration of their belonging to the common tradition, rather than 'a nearly Jeffersonian conception of the equality of states' (R.P. Toby, *op.cit.*, p. 221). Here the world is again seen in the light of a dichotomy, that we can designate as 'Asian countries–countries of Christendom'.

The mentality founded on the vertical structural principle attaches primary importance to the 'superior–inferior' relation, and very little, if any to the relation of parity. The world that is believed to consist of civilised centre and barbarian periphery, cannot embrace peer partners. If we underestimate this fact, then it would be possible to assert that Asami Keisai, for example, has understood the world 'as a number of independent states' (Sajja A. Prasad, *op.cit.*, p. 39) or to ascribe to him a 'neutral approach' due to the usage of 'objective terminology' like 'our country' and 'other country' (K.W. Nakai, *op.cit.*, p. 184). We want to focus attention on the latter judgement, that can be argued from two standpoints.

First of all, let us cite the following passage of Asami Keisai, where he proposes to use the terms 'our country' (*wagakuni*) and 'other country' (*ikoku*). He writes: 'If to consider our country as "inner" and others as "outer", if to make clear the meaning of "inner–outer", "guest–host", then using the terms "our country" and "other country" would not contradict anyone's logic (*sujimichi*)' (Asami Keisai, *Chūgoku ben* (Discussing the concept of Middle Kingdom), in *Nihon shisō taikei*, Vol. 31, p. 419). Here Asami Keisai mentions three pairs: 'inner–outer', 'guest–host', 'our–other', understood as relationships of one range. As correlated pairs they are used more than once. For example maintaining that if there did not exist the division between host–guest, this–that (*shukaku arekore hedate nakereba . . .*), it would become evident that the Way is the Way of our world (*ibid.*, p. 417). All these pairs can be interpreted as the forms of realisation of a fundamental opposition of traditional culture – the opposition 'own–alien', dominating in any ritual and determining its formal structure (A.I. Baiburin, 'Ritual: *svoyo i chujoe*' (Ritual: own and alien), in '*Folklor i etnografia. Problemi rekonstrukcii traditsionoi kulturi*' (Folklore and ethnography. Problems of reconstruction of traditional culture), ed. B.N. Putilov, Moscow, 1990, p. 16). This opposition can be expressed in various forms such as alive–dead, inner–outer, centre–periphery. In my opinion the pair 'our country–other country' can also be attributed to the same range, because if by itself the relation 'our–other' is not necessarily an opposition, in our case it can be defined as opposition, since the term used here for 'other' has a number of meanings such as 'strange, different, unusual, uncommon, queer' and is more close to 'alien' than to 'other'. Hence it belongs to the same range as the opposition 'centre–periphery'. Formally the opposition 'our–other' can be designated as more objective, whereas in content it seems to be not very distinct from the 'centre–periphery', discussed above.

On the other hand we must take into account that, as Nakane Chie has noted, in a society organised on the basis of the vertical principle, the consciousness of the difference between 'us' and 'them' is heightened, and it may develop to an extreme degree, when anyone outside 'our' people ceases to be considered human (Nakane Chie, *op.cit.*, p. 21). If we assume the concept of the vertical principle as the structural basis of the outer world view, then we have to recognise that relation 'our–other' fits the framework of the dichotomy 'The Middle Kingdom (centre) – barbarians (periphery)'. The idea of parity of states could not have appeared in the framework of the traditional outer world view (sinocentric or Japan-centred) founded on the vertical structural principle. Despite all the variations, the perception of the external world was based on the traditional dichotomy 'centre–periphery', a dichotomy modelled on the pattern of 'superior–inferior'.

**2**

# The Meiji Restoration: Japan's attempt to inherit China

**BEN-AMI SHILLONY**

## MING LOYALISM AND JAPANESE NATIONALISM

THE MEIJI RESTORATION is usually described as having followed two models, that of the contemporary West and that of Japan's Imperial past, while the third model, that of Imperial China, which for more than a thousand years had inspired the Japanese, is often believed to have been discarded. Yet a closer look at the concepts and symbols of the Meiji era suggests that although many Chinese ideas had indeed been abandoned, in other cases not only did the Chinese patterns hold their ground, but a further sinification occurred in them after the Meiji Restoration. This happened when the Meiji leaders, wishing to make Japan into the leading force of East Asia, adopted Chinese Imperial trappings which had not previously existed in Japan.

The self-image of Japan as the heir of China had already appeared in the middle of the seventeenth century when the Ming Empire was overthrown by the Manchu. The contrast between war-torn and 'barbarian'-ruled China and peaceful and orderly Japan suggested that not only had the rulers of China forfeited the mandate of heaven, but that China itself had lost that mandate to Japan. In this way Tokugawa Japan appeared as the legitimate heir of Ming China.

Scholars had traditionally been regarded in China as interpreters of the will of heaven, so when several Confucian scholars fled China and settled in Japan after the fall of the Ming, this was interpreted in Japan as a proof that China had lost the mandate of heaven which was transferred to Japan. About 20 Chinese scholars found refuge in Japan between the fall of the Ming in 1644 and the ascendence of the Kang Xi Emperor, a great patron of scholars, in 1661. They included Chin Genbin (Chinese: Chen Yuanyun, 1587–1671), who introduced Chinese martial arts into

Japan; Itsunen (Chinese: Yisan, 1601–1668), who introduced a new style of Chinese painting; and Ingen (Chinese: Yinyuan, 1592–1673), who established the Obaku Zen sect in Japan.[1]

Foremost among the Chinese who settled in Japan was Shu Shunsui (Zhu Shunshui, 1600–1682), a Confucian scholar from Yuyao, Zhejiang Province, the town where Wang Yangmin was born. After repeated failures to organise anti-Manchu fronts in Annam, South China and Japan, he was allowed to settle in Nagasaki in 1659. In 1665 Tokugawa Mitsukuni (1628–1700), the Lord of Mito and a grandson of Ieyasu, invited Shu to Edo to serve as his tutor and adviser. Shu stayed in Edo until his death 17 years later, making occasional trips to Mito and acquiring many disciples.[2]

Tokugawa Mitsukuni was engaged at that time in the monumental project of assembling a group of scholars to compile the history of Japan (*Dai Nihonshi*), on the model of the official Chinese histories. It was the same time that the Kang Xi Emperor was assembling scholars to compile the *Ming History* (Chinese: *Ming shi*). Mitsukuni was happy to enlist the expertise of a Chinese scholar like Shu for compiling the history of Japan. Shu had a deep impact on Mitsukuni and on some of the scholars who compiled the *Dai Nihonshi*. In 1693 his disciple Asaka Tampaku (1656–1737) was appointed head of the Shōkōkan, the bureau in charge of compiling the history. Through Asaka and other scholars Shu influenced the Mito school as well as the School of National Learning (*kokugaku*) which developed from it.

Being himself a refugee from what he deemed an illegitimate regime in China, Shu Shunsui was interested in the question, always of importance to Chinese historians, of the legitimacy of dynasties. As Japan had no Imperial dynastic changes, the only incident in Japanese history which somehow resembled the overthrow of the Ming was the overthrow of the southern branch of Emperor Godaigo in 1336 and its replacement by Emperors of the northern branch. The Mito school, with Shu Shunsui's support, acknowledged the Southern Court between 1336 and 1392, the years that the schism existed, as the legitimate one, despite the fact that the Emperors who followed, including those of the Tokugawa period, were descendants of the Northern Court.[3]

Shu expressed his support for the Southern Court in a colophon he wrote on a picture of Kusunoki Masashige, the loyal warrior who fought and died for Emperor Godaigo. In 1670, upon the request of Maeda Tsunanori (1643–1724), the daimyo of Kaga, Shu wrote the colophon on the picture of Kusunoki that the artist Kano Tanyu (1602–1674) had painted for Maeda. In this, Shu described Kusunoki as 'an exceptionally loyal, brave, honest and passionate gentleman', who 'skilfully restored the Imperial house'.[4] Mitsukuni was so impressed by the eulogy that in 1692, ten years after Shu's death, he erected a stone monument for Kusunoki at Minatogawa near Kobe, the site where Kusunoki had died in battle, and on that monument he engraved Shu Shunsui's words.[5]

Shu settled in Japan because he refused to recognise the legitimacy of the Qing, but in doing so he lent credit to the idea that Japan was the only country where Confucian ideals could be fully implemented. Indeed, in a letter to Tokugawa Mitsukuni, Shu wrote that because China could no longer achieve the great principle of harmony (大同, Chinese: dadung; Japanese: daidō), it was for Japan, under such benevolent rulers as Mitsukuni, to realise that ideal.[6] In this strange way the China-centred concept of loyalty to the Ming developed into the Japan-oriented idea that Tokugawa Japan, rather than Qing China, was the legitimate heir of the Ming. Yamaga Sokō (1622–1685), who had attended Shu's lectures in Edo and was influenced by him, wrote that Japan, being superior to China in all fields, was the true Central Kingdom (chūgoku).[7]

This nationalistic twist was totally different from the fate of Ming loyalism in Korea after the fall of the Ming. In Korea, which had remained part of the Chinese political system, loyalty to the Ming meant spiritual attachment to the deposed dynasty and a cherished anticipation of its future resurrection.[8] Thus, as Ronald Toby put it when describing Japan's foreign policy during the Tokugawa period, while Korea remained dependent on China, Japan was playing China.[9]

Despite the fact that under the rule of the Ming, Chinese and Japanese armies fought each other on the Korean peninsula during the Hideyoshi invasions of 1592–1598, after the fall of the Ming a nostalgic fascination with that dynasty spread in Japan. The play The Battle of Coxinga (Kokusenya kassen) by Chikamatsu Monzaemon (1655–1724) was one of the greatest hits of the Tokugawa period. Performed first in Osaka in 1715 as a puppet show, it was later adapted into *kabuki* and *noh*. The play depicts the Ming-loyalist warrior Coxinga (real name: Zhen Chenggong, 1624–1662), whose father was Chinese and whose mother was Japanese, as a Japanese hero by the name of Watōnai (literally meaning 'between Japan and China'). The message of the play is that only a Japanese warrior, carrying the blessings of the gods of Japan, can save China from its dire predicament.[10] An interest in the Ming appeared also in the field of jurisprudence. In the eighteenth century Ming legal codes were studied and applied in various *han*. In the 1720s Ogyū Sorai (1666–1728) and his younger brother Ogyū Kan (Hokkei, 1673–1744) published annotated editions of the Ming codes.[11]

The encroachment of the West in the nineteenth century produced the nationalist movement of *sonnō jōi* (usually translated as 'revere the Emperor, expel the barbarians', but literally meaning 'respecting the monarch, repelling the barbarians'). This slogan represented a traditional Chinese ideal, already stated by the historian Sima Qien (Ssu-ma Ch'ien) in the second century BC, that the duty of a governor was to respect the Emperor and repel the barbarians.[12] In the seventeenth century the Korean Ming loyalists created the slogan 'revere the Ming, expel the barbarians' (*chon-Myŏng yang-i*) to express their antagonism toward the Qing.[13] Thus the Japanese slogan was a paraphrase of the one coined by the Ming loyalists of Korea.

The Tokugawa rulers accepted the Chinese ideal that revering the monarch and repelling the barbarians were important moral duties, but they interpreted this as a confirmation of their policy of respecting the Emperor and closing the country to foreigners. The first one to use the term *jōi* in the sense of confronting the Westerners was Aizawa Seishisai (1782–1863) of the Mito school, who in his 1825 treatise *Shinron* developed the idea that Japan should respond to the Western threat by increasing its military power.[14] The phrase *sonnō jōi* was first used in the manifesto of the Mito school, the *kōdōkan-ki* of 1838, drafted by Fujita Tōko (1806–1855). At that time the phrase was not a revolutionary slogan, as it described the official policy of the Bakufu. It was only after the opening of Japan in 1854 that the slogan assumed a revolutionary, anti-shogunate meaning. Yoshida Shōin (1830–1859) used it to exhort loyalty to the Emperor, to urge the overthrow of the Bakufu, and to call for the expulsion of foreigners. Like Shu

Shunsui, Yoshida regarded loyalty to the legitimate monarch as the highest moral value (*taigi meibun*), and lamented the usurpation of the legitimate monarch's power by others. Like Shu, Yoshida admired Kusunoki Masashige. When passing the monument for Kusunoki at Minatogawa, he would read the inscription composed by Shu Shunsui and cry.[15] Like Yamaga Sokō, Yoshida referred to Japan as the Central Kingdom (*chūgoku*) or the Central Flower (*chūka*), two terms that had traditionally designated China.[16]

## CHINESE MODELS FOR THE MEIJI RESTORATION

The idea of restoring the fortunes of a legitimate but temporarily weakened dynasty was a classical Chinese concept. In the early 1860s, shortly before the Meiji Restoration, the Qing dynasty was 'restored' by a group of vigorous leaders who suppressed the Taiping and Nian rebellions, stopped foreign intervention, and modernised the armed forces. This was the Dongzhi (*t'ung-chih*) Restoration (*Dongzhi zhungxing*, Japanese: *Dōji chūkō*), called after the era name Dongzhi (1862–1875). The term *zhungxing* (Japanese: *chūkō*), or restoration, had been previously used to describe the revival of the Han dynasty in the first century and the revival of the Tang dynasty in the eighth century. In Japan it was used to designate the short restoration of Imperial powers by Emperor Godaigo between 1333 and 1336 (*Kemmu chūkō*).

In the *bakumatsu* period there was talk of restoring the declining fortunes of the shogunate. In 1857 Iwase Tadanari (1818–1861), one of the officials who conducted the talks with Townsend Harris, advised the shogun to open Japan in order to achieve a restoration (*chūkō isshin*) of the Bakufu.[17] The Meiji leaders first referred to their revolution as *ōsei fukko* (Chinese: *wangsheng fugu*), i.e. restoring the old monarchy, and later as *isshin* (Chinese: *yixin*), i.e. renovation, but these too were classical Chinese terms. The term *ishin* (Chinese: *weixin*), which was adopted in 1872 as part of the phrase *Meiji ishin* and which has designated the Meiji Restoration since then, was taken from the Chinese Book of Odes, where it referred to the restoration of the Zhou dynasty by King Wen in the twelfth century BC.[18]

The goal of the Meiji Restoration, to establish a centralised state, administered by a bureaucracy of merit, was a classical Chinese ideal that had for long been practised in China but hardly ever in Japan. The new status of the Emperor, as a sacrosanct, absolute monarch who ruled by decrees, exhortations and personal example, followed the classical Chinese model. It was different from the model of Europe at that time, where Emperors were limited by constitutions, as well as from that of Japan in the Nara and Heian periods, when Emperors were manipulated by aristocratic families.

At the beginning of the nineteenth century, several new or long forgotten Chinese practices started to be employed by the Imperial court, as part of the Tokugawa policy to provide the Emperors with a more China-like and therefore a more august image. This was done in order that the shoguns, who ruled in the name of the Emperors, could bask in the increased Imperial glory. Thus Emperor Go-Mizuno (r. 1771–1779) was the last Emperor to carry a posthumous Japanese name. The Japanese names of Emperors, like Mizuno or Sakuramachi, indicated places of residence and had no meritorious meaning. But from Go-Mizuno's successor Emperor Kōkaku (meaning 'bright character', r. 1780–1817) until today all Emperors have been given Chinese posthumous names with meritorious meanings, as was customary in China. Kōkaku was the last Emperor not to succeed his father and the last one to abdicate the throne, two long-practised Japanese traditions. From his son Emperor Ninkō (meaning 'benevolent filial piety', r. 1817–1846) until today all Emperors have reigned until they died and the reign has been transmitted directly in the Chinese way from father to son. Kōkaku was also the first Emperor after almost one thousand years to be accorded the posthumous title *tennō*. Until then the title had been *in*.[19]

In 1873 the Japanese government started using the term *kōtei* (Chinese: *huangdi*) for the Emperor in its correspondence with China and Korea. This term, hitherto reserved for the Emperors of China, had rarely been used in the past for the Emperors of Japan.[20] The fact that the Japanese now dared to do so meant that they regarded their Emperor as occupying the position that had once been occupied by the Emperors of China.

A similar message was conveyed by the new titles given to the peers in 1884. While the English equivalents of these titles (prince, marquis, count, viscount, baron) were adopted from the European aristocracy, the Japanese terms (*kō, haku, shi, dan*) were taken from Imperial China. China was also the model of the initial legal reform. The first criminal code (*kari keiretsu*), promulgated in 1868, was based on the Ming code. It remained in force until 1882, when it was remodelled after that of France.[21]

On 23 October 1868 almost two years after Emperor Mutsuhito had ascended the throne (he succeeded his father Emperor Kōmei in January 1867), the name of the era was changed from Keiō to Meiji. Changing the era after the accession ceremony (*sokui no rei*) of a new Emperor, a ceremony performed at least a year after the demise of the former Emperor, had been an established practice in Japan. It was therefore natural that one week after the accession ceremony of Mutsuhito, which took place in Kyoto on 16 October 1868, a new era would be proclaimed. The novel thing was that together with the change of eras it was announced that henceforth eras would coincide with Imperial reigns.[22] This principle of 'one reign, one era' (*issei ichigen*) had never existed in Japan before, as eras used to be changed on various occasions; and of course it had nothing to do with counting years in the West. This was a Chinese practice, started in 1368, exactly 500 years earlier, with the establishment of the Ming dynasty, and later followed by the Qing. During the Tokugawa period some Japanese scholars, like Nakai Chikuzan (1730–1804), advocated adopting the Chinese system, so that Japanese Emperors would, as in China, be known to posterity by the name of their reign.[23] But only during the Meiji Restoration was this system adopted in Japan.

The name Meiji which was chosen for the new era means 'enlightened rule'. The word suited the goals of the Meiji leaders, and fitted the idea of *bummei kaika* (enlightenment) which was propagated at that time. According to the Kido diary and other sources, the name of the era was chosen when the Emperor drew a lot out of several suggestions put before him by the councillor Matsudaira Shunsaku (1828–1890), the Lord of Fukui (Echizen).[24] Like the names of the previous eras this too was picked from the Chinese, rather than from the Japanese, classics. The name Meiji was adopted from a passage in the *Yijing* (*I Ching*), which states that the Sages in ruling (*ji*) turned to what was bright (*mei*).[25]

Yet Meiji can also mean Ming rule, a phrase which would fit the idea of inheriting China. There is no evidence that the Meiji leaders ever discussed such a meaning, but the character *mei* might have had an additional appeal to them by also signifying the Ming. The name Meiji also closely resembled the Chinese compound *dongzhi*, i.e. unified rule, which was the era in China at the time of the Meiji Restoration. Thus the era in which Japan became the leading state in East Asia carried a name which signified both Westernisation and a symbolic association with China.

## DONNING THE TRAPPINGS OF IMPERIAL CHINA

On 3 September 1868, one month before the era was changed, the name of Edo, the capital of the Tokugawa shoguns and the largest city in Japan, was changed to Tōkyō, initially also pronounced Tōkei. In November, for the first time in history, the Emperor visited that city and in the following April he returned to it, making it his permanent residence. The Chiyoda castle, where the shoguns had lived, was made into the Imperial palace. Tōkyō means 'eastern capital', but naming a capital by the direction of its location had no precedent in Japanese history. The country where such a practice had existed was China, which since the beginning of the Ming dynasty had had a Northern Capital (Beijing) and a Southern Capital (Nanjing), both established by the Ming.

In the eighteenth century some Japanese scholars wishing to imitate China, started referring to Edo as Tōkyō, but this was discouraged as the Imperial capital remained in Kyoto.[26] Changing the name of Edo to Tokyo (Chinese: Dongjing) in 1868 signified that the Emperor had been transferred from Western Japan to Eastern Japan. But in a broader sense it could also signify that the locus of leadership of East Asia had shifted from the northern and southern capitals of China to the Eastern Capital of Japan.

In June 1868 the former shogunal domain was divided into metropolitan districts (*fu*) and prefectures (*ken*), and in August 1871, following the abolition of the *han*, the whole country was redivided into *fu* and *ken*. Neither of these units had existed in Japan before. They both derived from China, where they stood for subdivisions of provinces: a province was divided into prefectures (*fu*), a prefecture was divided into subprefectures (*zhou*), and a subprefecture was divided into districts (*xian*, Japanese: *ken*). The new prefectural system (*fukensei*) of Japan, established in the early Meiji years, was thus a simplified version of the Chinese provincial division. As in China the governors of both the metropolitan districts and the prefectures were

27

appointed by the Emperor.

Another case of adopting a Chinese term after the Meiji Restoration was in 1871 when the yen (actually *en*, Chinese: *yuan*) was established as the new monetary unit, replacing the various units that had been in use before. The yen had never existed in Japan. It was taken from China, where it stood for the Mexican dollar, which was then the international monetary unit in East Asia. Indeed the Japanese yen was equivalent to the Mexican dollar. The word yen was pronounced the same way as the Chinese *yuan*, although the characters were different.

The Chinese model was also followed when Meiji Japan denied women the right to ascend the Imperial throne. Before the Meiji Restoration women could become Emperors in Japan, unlike in China where only males could be Emperors. There were six female Emperors in the seventh and eighth centuries, and there were two more female Emperors in the Edo period (Meishō, r. 1629–1643; and Gosakuramachi, r. 1762–1771). Restoring the status of the ancient Imperial institution should have meant reviving the tradition of female Emperors. This would also have fit the Western model, as the British monarch during most of the Meiji era was Queen Victoria. But the Meiji Constitution of 1889, for the first time in Japanese history, banned women from ascending the throne. Article 2 of the constitution stated: 'The Imperial Throne shall be succeeded by Imperial male descendants.' Japan thus adopted an Imperial Chinese principle which negated the Western model as well as its own Imperial tradition. A Japan with a woman *tennō* could not be the heir of China. Ironically, during most of the Meiji era the Chinese throne was controlled by a woman, the Empress dowager Zixi (Tz'u-hsi).

Meiji Japan also 'played China' in the field of language. Modernisation required adopting many Western terms that had to be incorporated into the Japanese language. Theoretically there were three ways of doing it: the Japanese could adopt the Western words in their original form by transcribing them in katakana, as they did later with many loan words; they could invent new words in the native Japanese language (*Yamato kotoba*); and they could create new Chinese words by either inventing new compounds or by giving new meanings to existing compounds. The Japanese preferred the third option, creating hundreds of new Chinese words and giving new and modern meanings to many existing Chinese words.[27]

Among the new Chinese words that they created were: *shakai* (*shehui*) for society; *kagaku* (*gexue*) for science; *keizai* (*jingji*) for economy; *tetsugaku* (*zhexue*) for philosophy; and *kakumei* (*geming*) for revolution. The Chinese language bestowed respectability on the Western concepts, and the Chinese ideographs made them self-explanatory, so that when the Chinese themselves embarked on their intensive modernisation a few decades later, they adopted most of the new Chinese words that the Japanese had created for them. The fact that the Japanese dared to invent a new Chinese vocabulary for the Western concepts shows that they regarded themselves heirs not only to the Chinese Empire but also to the Chinese language.

JAPANESE IMPERIALISM: CHINA INHERITED

Japanese imperialism was the epitome of the dream to inherit China. The new order that Meiji Japan constructed in East Asia was centred on Japan as the leader and on China as its satellite. Acquiring the historical Chinese dependencies the Ryukyu Islands and Korea, and incorporating them into the Japanese Empire, had therefore a great symbolic significance for Japan.[28]

Already in the Tokugawa period there were Japanese who referred to their country as *Dai Nihon* (Great Japan), on the Chinese model of *Da Ming* (Great Ming) and *Da Qing* (Great Qing), and the sinophile philosopher Ogyū Sorai even refused to call China *Da Qing*.[29] After the Meiji Restoration the official name of Japan became *Dai Nihon Teikoku* (Empire of Great Japan). This fitted the Chinese model of *Da Qing* as well as the Western model of 'Great Britain'. At the same time the common appellation for China in Japan ceased to be *chūgoku* (Central Kingdom) and became *Shina*, a name derived from the Western word 'China' which carried no associations with importance or centrality.[30]

Japan's contempt for China reached a peak during the Sino-Japanese War of 1894–1895, in which Japan proved its superiority by defeating the Chinese army and navy. In the Shimonoseki Treaty the Japanese gained possession of Taiwan and detached Korea from China. After making Taiwan their colony, they built a shrine for Coxinga there, where the half-Japanese Ming loyalist warrior could now be worshipped as a Shinto god.[31]

At the end of the nineteenth century, Chinese reformists and revolutionaries like Kang Yuwei (1858–1927), Liang Qichao (1873–1929), and Sun Yat-sen (1866–1925) started looking to Japan as a model for China, in the same way that the Japanese had once been looking to China as a model for Japan. These Chinese reformists also rediscovered Shu Shunsui, who like them had sought refuge in Japan from an oppressive Qing government. Thus Shu Shunsui, who until then had hardly been known in China, became also famous in his native country.[32]

In June 1912, shortly before the death of the Meiji Emperor and the end of the Meiji era, a monument commemorating the 250th anniversary of Shu's arrival in Japan was erected on the grounds of the First Higher School (*ichikō*) in Tokyo, the site of the former Mito residence where Shu Shunsui had once lived. At the ceremony which was then held, the education minister and members of the Tokugawa and Maeda families praised the Chinese scholar who had made Japan his second home.[33] By then the dream of inheriting China had almost been realised: Japan had become the leading country of East Asia, Taiwan and Korea were its colonies, and the *tennō* was the only Emperor under heaven in that part of the world.

## NOTES

1. Tsuji Zennosuke, *Kaigai kōtsū shiwa* (Tokyo: Naigai Shoseki, 1930), pp. 660–3. For the place of China[21] in Tokugawa Japan, see Marius B, Jensen, *China in the Tokugawa World* (Cambridge: Harvard University Press, 1992).
2. For the story of Shu Shunsui in Japan see Ishihara Michihiro, *Shu Shunsui* (Tokyo: Yoshikawa Kobunkan, 1961); Yamamoto Takeo, 'Shunsui, Dokuryū, Seian', *Nihon Rekishi*, 218 (July 1966), pp. 51–2; Julia Ching, 'Chu Shun-shui, 1600–82, a Chinese Confucian scholar in Tokugawa Japan', *Monumenta Nipponica*, XXX, 2 (summer 1975), pp. 177–91.
3. For the *Dai Nihonshi* attitude to the Southern Court see Kate Wildman Nakai, 'Tokugawa Confucian Historiography: The Hayashi, Early Mito School, and Arai Hakuseki', in Peter Nosco (ed.), *Confucianism and Tokugawa Culture* (Princeton: Princeton University Press, 1984), pp. 62–91.
4. Bito Masahide, 'Sonnō jōi shiso', in *Iwanami kōza Nihon rekishi* (Tokyo: Iwanami Shoten, 1977), Vol, 13, p. 62. See also Warren W. Smith, *Confucianism in Modern Japan* (Tokyo: Hakuseido Press, 1973), p. 33.
5. Ishihara, *Shu Shunsui*, p. 239.
6. Inaba Iwakichi (Kunsan), *Shu Shunsui Zenshu* (Tokyo: Kyōkaidō

Shoten, 1912), pp. 59–60, quoted in Ishihara, *Shu Shunsui*, pp. 200–1.
7. For Yamaga's usage of *chūgoku* see Bito, '*Sonnō jōi*, p. 50–1. Ronald P. Toby, *State and Diplomacy in Early Modern Japan* (Princeton: Princeton University Press, 1984), pp. 222–6; Nakai, *Tokugawa Confucian Historiography*, p. 187.
8. For Ming loyalism in Korea see Sato Seizaburo, 'Response to the West: The Korean and Japanese Patterns', in Albert Craig (ed.), *Japan: A Comparative View* (Princeton: Princeton University Press, 1979), pp. 115–17; Toby, *State and Diplomacy*, 224 n. 138, 228.
9. Toby, *State and Diplomacy*, p. 229.
10. For the play *Kokusenya kassen* see Donald Keene, *The Battles of Coxinga* (Cambridge: Cambridge University Press, 1971).
11. Ch'en, Paul Heng-chao, *The Formation of the Early Meiji Legal Order* (Oxford: Oxford University Press, 1981), pp. 9–10.
12. David M. Earl, *Emperor and Nation in Japan*, (Seattle: University of Washington Press, 1964), p. 105.
13. Sato, 'Response', p. 115.
14. Herschel Webb, *The Japanese Imperial Institution in the Tokugawa Period* (New York: Columbia University Press, 1968), pp. 214–15. Bob T. Wakabayashi, *Anti-Foreignism and Western Learning in Early Modern Japan*. (Cambridge: Council on East Asian Studies, Harvard University, 1986), pp 51–7.
15. H.D. Harootunian, *Toward Restoration* (Berkeley: University of California Press, 1970), pp. 184–5; *Shu Shunsui* (Tokyo: Shu Shunsui Kinenkai Jimusho, 1912), pp. 35–6.
16. H. Van Straelan, *Yoshida Shoin: Forerunner of the Meiji Restoration* (Leiden: E.J. Brill, 1952), p. 53.
17. Henry D. Smith, 'The Edo–Tokyo Transition: In Search of a Common Ground', in Marius B. Jansen and Gilbert Rozman (eds), *Japan in Transition* (Princeton: Princeton University Press, 1986), pp. 352–3.
18. Webb, *The Imperial Japanese Institution*, p. 200.
19. Fujita Satoru, 'Tennō-gō no saikō', in Irokawa Daikichi *et al.*, *Tennōsei* (Tokyo: Kawade Shobō Shinsha, 1990), pp. 94–8; Sugimoto Fumiko, 'Tennō-gō o megutte', *Rekishi hyōron*, 457 (May 1988), pp. 43–7.
20. Sugimoto, 'Tennō-gō', p. 45. On 18 April 1936, with the rise of ultra-nationalism and the further decline of China's prestige in Japan, the title of the Japanese Emperor in Chinese was changed back from *Nihon koku kōtei* to *Dai Nihon teikoku tennō*.
21. Ch'en, *The Formation*, pp. 9–10, 17, 21–3.
22. Matsushima Eiichi, 'Issei ichigen no nengō ni tsuite', in Nagahara Keiji and Matsushima Eiichi, (eds), *Gengō mondai no honshitsu* (Tokyo: Hakuseki Shoten, 1979), p. 97.
23. Sugimoto, 'Tennō-gō', p. 47; *Nihon kōshitsu jiten* (Tokyo: Rekishi Hyakki, 1979), p. 306.
24. Kido Takayoshi, *The Diary of Kido Takayoshi* (tr. Sidney D. Brown and Akiko Hirata. Tokyo: University of Tokyo Press, 1983), I, 112; *Nihon kōshitsu jiten*, p. 306.
25. *Nihon kōshitsu jiten*, p. 26. The quote from the *Yijing* is from *shuo kua IV*. The English translation appears in Richard Wilhelm, *The I Ching or Book of Changes* (tr. Cary F. Baynes. Princeton: Princeton University Press, 1983), p. 269.
26. Herman Ooms, *Tokugawa Ideology: Early Constructs, 1570–1680*

(Princeton: Princeton University Press, 1985), p. 162.

27. Roy A. Miller, *The Japanese Language* (Chicago: Chicago University Press, 1967), pp. 259–62.

28. For Japanese attempts to achieve part of this goal already in the Tokugawa period, see Toby, *State and Diplomacy*.

29. Kate Wildman Nakai, 'The Naturalisation of Confucianism in Tokugawa Japan: The Problems of Sinocentrism', *Harvard Journal of Asiatic Studies*, XL, 1 (June 1980), p. 182.

30. Kate Wildman Nakai, *Shogunal Politics: Arai Hakuseki and the Premises of Tokugawa Rule* (Cambridge: Council on East Asian Studies, Harvard University, 1988), p. 324; Harry D. Harootunian, 'The Function of China in Tokugawa Thought', in Akira Iriye (ed.), *The Chinese and the Japanese* (Princeton: Princeton University Press, 1980), p. 27.

31. Keene, *The Battles of Coxinga*, p. 85.

32. Ching, *Chu Shun-sui*, p. 178.

33. *Shu Shunsui*; Ishihara, *Shu Shunsui*, pp. 252–3. Actually the 250th anniversary was three years earlier.

# Soviet–Japanese studies on the problem of the Meiji Ishin and the development of capitalism in Japan

## JULIA MIKHAILOVA

THE HISTORICAL EVENTS of 1867–8, known by the name of Meiji Ishin were the central point of Japan's modern history and defined to a great extent the further development of the country. Hence, the research on such an important subject reflects not only the main tendencies of Soviet Japanese studies, but of Soviet historical studies in general.

It is possible to single out three periods of these studies: 1920–30, 1950–70 and the 1980s. The first was the period of emergence of the Marxist historical school in the Soviet Union. All studies in humanities at that time were imbued with vulgar economical determinism, superfluous sociologisation and an approach to history from the viewpoint of class struggle. Concerning the Meiji Ishin, this mode of research presupposed that a revolution could be called bourgeois only where it had the bourgeoisie as its leading force and an agrarian revolution as an integral part. So, the solution to the problem was limited by the dichotomy: revolution or reform.

Two books may serve as good illustrations of the point. The first one *The History of the Meiji Era* was written by O.V. Pletner at the beginning of the 1920s. (The exact year of publication is unknown.) Characterising the Meiji Ishin, Pletner wrote 'We may conclude that Japan, having changed its economical structure, still did not possess the class of bourgeoisie which could take over the rule of the country. It was the class of feudal lords that remained in power. They acknowledged the changes which had happened in Japan, rejected all outmoded feudal norms and started the rapid development of capitalism on the new economic basis. . .

Hence, the term "revolution" may be used in relation to the Meiji Ishin only conventionally. It may be called "bourgeois" only from the viewpoint of its results, which does not mean at all that the bourgeoisie played the most important role at that time'.[1]

Another Soviet scholar V.S. Svetlov in his book *Origins of Capitalistic Japan* criticised the approach to Meiji Ishin as a revolution, carried out under the guidance of the Emperor. He considered these events to be the verge of feudalism and capitalism and thus acknowledged their importance. Like Pletner, Svetlov claimed that feudal lords, not the bourgeoisie, came into power in 1868 and viewed it as only a 'shift inside one and the same class'.[2] Meiji Ishin, he wrote, 'half-opened the doors for the development of industrial and financial capital, while the bourgeois state was not created'. In the end he called the Meiji Ishin a reform.

In the 1920s and 1930s Soviet studies of the Meiji Ishin were closely connected with the revolutionary and political struggle taking place in Japan at that time. In 1927 and 1932 the so-called *Comintern Theses on Japan* were published. Leaders of Comintern and the JCP, who wanted to prove that Japan was on the threshold of bourgeois-democratic revolution which would inevitably grow into a proletarian one, rejected the importance of the Meiji Ishin and refused to acknowledge the fact that it paved the way for capitalism. Their purpose was to promote revolutionary activities among the poor in their struggle against a reactionary political regime. The Soviet Union rejected the viewpoint of those Japanese Marxists who gave preference to legal, economical methods of struggle, who saw no possibility of victory for the revolutionary movement in Japan and who regarded the Meiji Ishin as a bourgeois revolution. On the whole, we should characterise the above-mentioned research as too abstract; they seem to be no more than the mechanical application of Marxist theory to Japanese reality.

The research by N. Wainzwaig[3] which unfortunately fell into oblivion in the years to follow was in complete contrast to these views. Written in 1934, it has many similarities with the contemporary research of Soviet Japanese scholars. Wainzwaig emphasised the following points in the development of Japanese capitalism. The crash of the Tokugawa shogunate occurred under the influence of the world market economy which Japan became involved in after its 'opening', but at the same time the preconditions had been ripening inside Japanese society itself. Japan began a period of bourgeois development when other capitalist countries were already entering the imperialistic stage. This enabled the Japanese to have a shorter period of industrial capitalism. The dominance of feudal and trade monopolies in the Tokugawa era and the absence of free competition in industry and trade were favourable to this path of development. Though Wainzwaig did not touch on the problem of the Meiji Ishin itself, on the whole he was the only one among the Soviet scholars of that time who approached Japanese history as having peculiarities of its own, not just copying the European way.

By the end of the 1930s an appraisal of the Meiji Ishin as an uncompleted bourgeois revolution became widely acknowledged by Soviet scholars, having as its basis the awareness of the need to pay more attention to the results of the events. This viewpoint is represented by the works of H. Ejdus and E. Zhukov.[4] Characterising the essence of the Meiji Ishin and of the reforms brought forth by it, Ejdus wrote 'These reforms were bourgeois in their essence and paved the way for the development of capitalism in Japan. Though the reforms were uncompleted and half-done, thanks to them Japan experienced political, economical and social change of great importance. Thus both from the viewpoint of the essence and the form the overturn of 1868 was a revolution'.[5]

Zhukov's *History of Japan* was a faithful compilation of the works of Western scholars though revised under the Marxist approach. Zhukov held several important positions in the academic circles of the Soviet Union, and it was probably due to this fact that his viewpoint remained dominant even in post-war Soviet Japanese studies. It is peculiar that while trying to prove the rightness of his assessment of the Meiji Ishin, Zhukov cited the words by V.I. Lenin, who called the events of 1867–1868 'revolution and reforms'. The custom of citing Marx and Lenin was widespread among the Soviet scholars up to recent times. The few remarks by 'Classics' about Japan were borrowed from work to work, though it was always hard to believe that Marx and Lenin understood Japanese history better than contemporary scholars.

After the war the efforts of scholars were primarily concentrated on revealing the beginnings of capitalist relations in Tokugawa Japan. The problem of the genesis of capitalism was central to the studies of an outstanding Soviet scholar, A. Galperin. He attributed the emergence of capitalist relations in Japan to the end of the sixteenth and beginning of the seventeenth centuries, emphasising the rapid development of towns, industrial production – especially mining, the growth of foreign and domestic trade, the appearance of a large number of peasants deprived of land due to the development of commodity–money relations.[6]

Concerning the Meiji Ishin he characterised these events as 'having revolutionary meaning, namely the meaning of the uncompleted bourgeois revolution'. In the course of these events [he wrote] the rule over the country passed from large-scale feudal lords to new elements who, being of samurai origin, represented the interests of the new capitalist class and with the support of the large-scale bourgeoisie carried out several reforms, bourgeois in their essence. The Revolution of 1868 remained uncompleted, half-done, but though a lot of feudal remnants still existed in the country, capitalist relations became dominant.[7]

The centenary of the Meiji Ishin stimulated discussion about its character among Soviet scholars. A symposium on the theme was held in the Institute of Oriental Studies and a number of articles by leading Japanologists were published. The main points of the discussion may be summarised as follows. Soviet scholars criticised those Japanese scholars (*Rōnōha*) who considered that the capitalist mode of production was introduced into the country from outside, after its 'opening'. They also rejected the viewpoint of the *Kōzaha* according to which the Meiji Ishin was understood as the creation of absolutism. Soviet Japanologists came to the conclusion that the starting point of the Meiji Ishin should be attributed to 1864–65 when the anti-Tokugawa coalition was formed and the end to the time of the completion of the reforms carried out by the Meiji government, particularly the land reforms of 1873, as that meant the formation of new social–economic relations.[8]

Many scholars emphasised the fact that in the period 1950–60 during the break-up of the colonial system and the search by Asian and African countries for ways of development, the problem of the Meiji Ishin acquired 'international importance'. The theory of modernisation became popular in world Japanese studies at that time and 'the Japanese way' of development was considered to be an example for those countries which had just gained their independence. But Soviet scholars deprived 'the Japanese experience' of any positive meaning, wishing to stress that the Japanese and other peoples of Asia payed a heavy price for rapid capitalist development.[9]

The weak point of all the studies, mentioned above, came out of the fact that the history of bourgeois revolution, the emergence of the capitalist mode of production and bourgeois state in Japan were analysed with the help of criteria used while researching the corresponding processes in well-developed capitalistic countries of the West. The facts of Japanese history were adjusted to fit into a certain scheme. Hence many difficulties in understanding Japanese history appeared. Most difficult to explain was the correlation of 'external' and 'internal' factors in the ripening of preconditions for the Meiji Ishin, of revolution from 'below' and reforms carried out by the Meiji government, the essence of state power, formed in the result of Meiji Ishin, etc. The term 'uncompleted revolution' was just a convenient device for 'explaining' the things which were difficult to understand.

In the 1980s the theory according to which the world community is to be analysed from the viewpoint of various models of capitalist development (classical, primary, secondary, tertiary) became widespread in the Soviet Union. Japan as well as Germany, Italy and Russia was considered to belong to the secondary model or to the so-called 'latecomers'. As noted in the book *Evolution of Eastern Societies: A Synthesis of Traditional and Contemporary Structures*,[10] the peculiarities of the development of 'latecomers' are rooted in their lagging behind the primary models of capitalism and, hence, in the objective necessity for shortening, reducing the stages of their further development. The authors of the book emphasised the positive and emphatic role of tradition in the process of capitalist development, which let the organic fusion of new European institutions and ideas with national Japanese, and the leading role of state which tried to 'superimpose' capitalism as quickly as possible, to mould and consolidate secular society. To my regret, this theory is more popular among the specialists in the history of other Asian countries than Japan. It has not yet been completely combined with the studies of Japanese history, based on thorough analysis of concrete historical data. So an outline of the history of the

Meiji Ishin has not yet been written in the Soviet Union.

## NOTES

1. Pletner, O. *The History of the Meiji Era*, p. 61.
2. Svetlov, V.S. *Origins of Capitalist Japan*. (Moscow, Leningrad, 1934) p. 111.
3. *Contemporary Japan. Collection of Works*, No. 2, 1934, pp. 178–218.
4. Ejdus, H. *Japan*. (Moscow, 1938); Zhukov, E. *History of Japan*. (Moscow, 1939).
5. Ejdus, H., *op.cit.*, p. 55.
6. Galperin, A.L. 'On the Problem of the Genesis of Capitalism in Japan'. *On the Genesis of Capitalism in Eastern Countries (15th–19th centuries)*. (Moscow, 1962) p. 8.
7. Galperin, A.L. 'Socio-economic Preconditions of the Bourgeois Revolution in Japan'. *Transactions of the Institute of Oriental Studies*. Vol. 23. Japan. (Moscow, 1959, p. 114.)
8. Leschenko, N.F. 'Soviet Historiography on Meiji Ishin and the Genesis of Capitalism in Japan'. *Russia and Japan in the Researches of Russian and Japanese Scholars*. (Moscow, 1986) pp. 46–7.
9. Zhukov, E. 'On the Problem of the Assessment of "Meiji Revolution"'. *Problems of History*. (1968) No. 2, p. 53.
10. *Evolution of Eastern Societies: A Synthesis of Traditional and Contemporary Structures*. (Moscow, 1986).

# 4

# Tradition as justification for change: History in the service of the Japanese government (1869–1893)

## MARGARET MEHL

THE MEIJI RESTORATION in 1868 marked the end of 250 years of Tokugawa rule. The changes that took place in Japan in the following years were so profound that some scholars have preferred the term 'revolution' to characterise the events of 1868.[1] However, the motto of the leaders of the Meiji Restoration was *fukko* (restoration, revival). They justified the overthrow of the Tokugawa Bakufu by calling for a return to Imperial government. To examine the question of legitimation as distinct from motives for the Meiji Restoration may contribute to our understanding of it and enable us to compare different types of legitimation in Japanese history and in Japan and other countries. For example, in Europe the general line of argument changes in the course of the seventeenth century from a return to a supposed old order to a breakthrough to a new order.[2]

The first new government institutions after 1868 were modelled after those that existed in the Nara period (710–784). They were gradually changed or replaced by institutions more suited to meet modern needs. Among the practices revived from the Nara period, official historiography in the tradition of the Six National Histories, the *Rikkokushi*, endured for longer than most. The first office established for the purpose in 1869 was soon abolished, but it had successors and from them emerged what is now the Historiographical Institute (*Tōkyō daigaku Shiryō hensanjo*).[3]

In my paper I want to show the parallels between the political changes and the history of official historiography in the beginning of the Meiji period and to suggest that there was a connection: historiography served to legitimate political reforms.

In 1868 the new government was modelled after the
*ritsuryō* state of the Nara period, when Imperial power was
at its height. At that time the *ritsuryō* laws formed the
political and legal base of the state while the Six National
Histories, *Rikkokushi*, provided a guide for Imperial rule on
the basis of Confucian morals. The historian Sakamoto Tarō
has pointed out that the last commentary on the *ritsuryō*
laws, the *Engishiki*, was completed at around the same time
as the last of the *Rikkokushi*, the *Sandai jitsuroku*.[4] Given
this close link between the Imperial bureaucratic state and
the compilation of a national history, it is not surprising that
the scholars who supported the Meiji Restoration sought to
revive historiography by the state. In February 1869 officials
of the *gakkō*, for former Bakufu academy *Shōheikō*, which
had been reopened as an administrative organ for education,
submitted a proposal to establish an office for the
compilation of a national history. Since the *Rikkokushi*,
the authors of the proposal claimed, there had been no
official history (*seishi*), but now that Imperial rule had been
revived the *Rikkokushi* should be continued. The proposal
was accepted and an office established in the *Wagaku
kōdansho* (Institute of Japanese Studies), another former
Bakufu institution. An Imperial rescript (*shūshi no choku*)
sanctioned the move with the same arguments as the ones in
the proposal. Scholars of National Studies (*kokugaku*) and
Chinese Studies (*kangaku*) were appointed for the task.
However the attempt was given up the same year and the
office closed.

In 1871 the abolition of the domains and the establishment of the prefectures (*haihan chiken*) marked a decisive
step towards the consolidation of power in the hands of the
central government. At around this time an official in the
Central Government Office (*dajōkan*), Nagamatsu Miki
(1834–1903), was ordered to compile a Chronicle of the
Meiji Restoration, the *Fukkoki*. Nagamatsu was a government official who, like some of the leaders of the Meiji
Restoration, came from the Chōshū Domain. The following
year a Department of History (*rekishika*) headed by
Nagamatsu Miki was established in the Council of State
(*dajōkan*), the highest executive organ of the Meiji
government. Beside work on the Chronicle of the Restoration its most important task was to collect materials
concerning the recent history of the prefectures. The
creation of a centralised state made it possible as well as

necessary to collect information concerning the different regions of the country, and probably the Department of History partly served to provide information as a basis for administration. At this time the compilation of a national history does not seem to have been attempted.

In 1875 the Osaka Conference ended a series of political crises. The unity of the government had collapsed after the return of the Iwakura Mission to America and Europe in 1873 and the growing People's Rights Movement (*jiyū minken undō*) posed a further threat. At the conference a compromise was reached; the Council of State was reorganised and on 14 April 1875 an Imperial rescript announced the gradual establishment of constitutional government. On the same day the Office of Historiography (*shūshikyoku*) was set up in place of the former Department of History. *Shūshi* means 'to write history', and the name of the new office indicates the intention to compile a national history. It seems significant that this change occurred after a power struggle among the Meiji leaders had resulted in further consolidation of the government while at the same time the necessity was felt to legitimate its power in the face of the People's Rights Movement.

From 1875 onwards the history of official historiography is fairly well documented and we have the first detailed information about who was in the Office of Historiography: probably the typical 'historiographer' was no different from other officials: most of them had been born around 1830 and educated in the Confucian tradition, often in part at the Bakufu academy *Shōheikō* in Edo; they had been politically active around the time of the Meiji Restoration; they came from those domains who helped to overthrow the Bakufu. Their appointment to the Office of Historiography was however often a sign of waning political influence.[5] Only gradually did some of those who stayed in the Office of Historiography become specialists; Shigeno Yasutsugu (1827–1910), who became deputy Director of the Office in September 1875, was soon the most influential member and became one of the first professional historians in Japan. The Office of Historiography had four departments: two of them collected and arranged source materials from the fourteenth century to the end of the Edo period (1600–1868), the third continued work on the Chronicle of the Restoration under Nagamatsu, who was also Director of the Office, and the fourth department collected sources prior to the fourteenth

41

century and examined the Imperial genealogies. The first two departments therefore worked on what was to become the basis of a national history. For the moment however, progress was slow. Although the Office performed other tasks besides those mentioned, it was abolished in 1877 and the College of Historiography (shūshikan) which replaced it had less personnel and a smaller budget. Nevertheless work continued as before until the College was completely reorganised in 1881.

The political events of 1881, the so-called Political Change, were similar to those in 1875 in that the government was threatened from disunity within and widespread protest from without. As the League for Founding a National Assembly (kokkai kisei dōmei), which had emerged from the former People's Rights Movement spread through the country, the Hokkaidō Colonisation Assets Scandal (haraisage jiken) provided fuel for opposition to the government. But before opposition inside and outside the government could unite, Ōkuma Shigenobu (1838–1922), who had campaigned for the immediate opening of a parliament, was expelled from the government. At the same time an Imperial edict announced that a parliament was to be opened in 1890 after the proclamation of a constitution. Itō Hirobumi became the most influential member of the government, which had once again secured the authority to determine the political fate of the country. In the following years, while preparing a constitution for Japan, the Meiji leaders attempted to contain the powers of a future parliament; the financial base of the Imperial household was secured; a new peerage was created, which was intended to form a majority in the future Upper House; the position of the bureaucracy was strengthened by laws to make it less dependent on short-term policies.

The reorganisation of the College of Historiography (shūshikan) was an immediate result of the political crisis of 1881. An anonymous memorandum mentions discontent with the work of the Academy and states that if it had nothing to show for it by the time the parliament began to debate on the budget it would probably lose its funding.[6] It seems that progress in the College was hampered not only by underfunding and too many different projects but also by the differences of opinion held by its members. In 1881 the organisation became more hierarchical and the compilation of a national history was named as the central aim. The history had the title *Dainihon hennenshi*, (*Chronological History of Great Japan*), it was to comprise the period from the beginning of the fourteenth century (the *Dainihonshi* of the Mito scholars having been recognised as a legitimate account of the preceding age) to the Meiji Restoration and to be written in the Sino-Japanese style (*kanbun*). Work on it was begun the following year. Thus, the official national history ordered by the Imperial rescript of 1869 was at last to be written, but the time at which this happened gave it a new significance. The *Dainihon hennenshi* became part of the preparations for the proclamation of the constitution; later sources indicate that it was to be completed by 1890.

The 'conservative eighties' saw a new emphasis on Japanese traditions as opposed to the Westernisation of the previous years; at Tokyo University (which became the first Imperial University in 1886) a special seminar for Chinese and Japanese Studies (*koten kōshūka*) was established in 1882, and in the same year an Institute for Japanese Philology (*Kōten kōkyū sho*) was founded (the present Kokugakuin University). Two new projects to compile a national history initiated in the following year 1883 show the importance accorded to history in this context. The *Shigaku kyōkai* (Historical Society) was founded by scholars of National Studies with the aim of writing a history of Japan in Japanese and comprising various aspects of Japanese tradition instead of merely the political development. The Society was presided over by Soejima Taneomi (1828–1905) and among its principal members was Konakamura Kiyonori (1821–1895) who had been in the first office for the compilation of a national history in 1869. The second project was initiated by Iwakura Tomomi (1825–1883), who set up an office in the Imperial household ministry where an account of Japan's political development centring around the Imperial line was compiled with the title *Taisei kiyō* (*Account of the Imperial Rule*). The compilers were members of the administration, Konakamura Kiyonori who taught at the Imperial University (now Tokyo University) being the only exception. The language was Japanese as opposed to the Sino-Japanese style of the *Dainihon hennenshi*. Iwakura planned to complete the account within six months, by which time the statesman Itō Hirobumi (1841–1909), who had just left for Europe to study constitutional laws, was expected to return. Translations of this history were to be prepared for the foreign advisors, so that in helping to draft a constitution they would take into account Japan's special qualities. In the *Taisei kiyō* the origins and the history of the Imperial institution were to be described; the aim was to show the historical legitimation of a strong Emperor under the new constitution.[7]

Iwakura Tomomi, one of the leaders of the Restoration, feared that a constitution based on foreign models would fail to be in accordance with Japanese traditions. He was not the only one to hold such a view. Miura Yasushi (1829–1910), who had been appointed inspector (*kanji*) at the College of Historiography in 1877, expressed a similar view in two memoranda submitted in 1880 and 1882.[8] In the first one, addressed to Sanjō Sanetomi, he emphasised the Emperor's role in the Meiji Restoration. Only the unique character of Japan's unbroken line of Emperors, argued Miura, made it possible for Imperial rule to be restored in such a short time. Now Japan was borrowing extensively from the West but there was the danger of throwing out the special qualities of the Japanese Empire (*kōkoku no koyū no gokokushitsu*) together with the bad customs of the past. For Miura the Emperor had to have a strong position under the new constitution which itself could only be granted by the Emperor. Likewise the people must be bound to the Emperor. A sense of crisis in the face of the movement for popular rights is evident from this memorandum; Miura criticised the opposition to the government and their use of Western concepts. He mentioned the death of some of the Meiji leaders, among them Ōkubo Toshimichi (1830–1878) who had been assassinated the year before, as another reason for strengthening the Imperial position.

Miura's second memorandum is addressed to Itō Hirobumi on the occasion of his journey to Europe to study the constitutions of European countries. The content is similar to that of the first memorandum. Miura described the changes that had taken place in Japan since the Restoration which from *fukko* (Restoration) had changed to *ishin* (Renovation). Then he made the following points: the movement for the establishment of a parliament looks mainly to England and France. However in those countries the democratic system resulted from opposition to the misrule of a monarch. In Japan, Imperial rule remains unbroken and it was the Emperor himself who proclaimed the opening of a parliament in ten years. Japan should therefore look to Prussia for an example as the German

Federal Empire had been founded by monarchs. Again Miura emphasised the unique character of Japan and its national policy (*kokutai*) and the necessity of taking it into account when drafting the constitution.

Itō Hirobumi was advised to keep the historical development of his country in mind while preparing the constitution for Japan not only by Miura, but also by Lorenz von Stein (1815–1890) whose lectures on constitutional history and law Itō had attended in Vienna in October 1882. Stein compared the constitutions of England, France, Austria and Prussia to demonstrate how different societies produced different constitutions.[9] Stein warned Japan against simply adopting the constitution of another country. In the winter of 1889, already on his deathbed, he advised Kaneko Kentarō (1853–1942), who had been Itō's interpreter, that Japan should publish its own constitutional history in Japan and abroad so that the nature of the Japanese constitution be better understood. He also stressed the importance of national history in education to foster the love of one's own country.

However it seems that the Japanese may not have needed this kind of advice. On the day the constitution was proclaimed, 11 February 1889, the historian Shigeno Yasutsugu, by then professor at the Imperial University, gave a lecture at a ceremony at the university entitled *Wagakuni korai no kenpō oyobi daigaku no keikyō* (The Constitution of Our Country since Ancient Times and the Situation of the University). In this lecture he compared two ancient legal texts, the 17 Articles of the year 604 and the Taihō code (701), with the Meiji Constitution and concluded that in essence the laws were similar, merely adapted to the times.[10] In the same month Shigeno published an essay on the causes of the Meiji Restoration in the magazine *Bun*.[11] According to Shigeno the causes dated as far back as the establishment of the Kamakura Shogunate by Minamoto Yoritomo in the twelfth century as this was when the usurpation of Imperial rule began. Among the immediate causes he emphasised the role of the scholars from the Mito Domain in demonstrating the legitimacy of Imperial rule in their *History of Great Japan* (*Dainihonshi*; begun in 1672 and finally completed in 1906).

Given this importance of history to legitimate change, especially Japan's first constitution, which borrowed heavily from Western models, what had in the meantime become of the official chronological history *Dainihon hennenshi*? As mentioned above, work on it had begun in 1882, and it continued throughout the 1880s. But the two additional attempts to write a definitive national history by the *Shigaku kyōkai* and by Iwakura Tomomi suggest discontent with the way Shigeno and his colleagues were doing their job. In fact other sources as well as the apologetic tone of memoranda by the College of Historiography support the impression. Two points were most widely criticised: the language of the *Dainihon hennenshi*, Sino-Japanese (*kanbun*), and the slow progress of its compilation.

When the cabinet system was introduced in 1885 the College of Historiography was renamed Temporary Office of Historiography (*rinji shushikyoku*). This suggests that the Office was soon to be abolished, probably before the proclamation of the constitution. The first draft of the Meiji Constitution was completed in April 1888 and revised in the following months. In October of that year, the president of the Imperial University, Watanabe Kōki (1848–1901) submitted a proposition to move the Office of Historiography to the university, in which he emphasised the need to study the history of Japan using scientific methods.[12] For him the study of history was essential to the understanding of law, economy and politics and as a basis for reform. The Office of Historiography would be an asset to the Department of Japanese History which was to be established following the Department of History (*shigakka*), established the year before.

Presumably the fate of the Office of Historiography had been discussed previously, for the move was effected that same month and the Office of Historiography became the Temporary Department for the Compilation of a Chronological History (*rinji hennenshi hensan kakari*) at the Imperial University, now known as the Historiographical Institute. Shigeno Yasutsugu and his colleagues Kume Kunitake (1839–1931) and Hoshino Hisashi (1839–1917) became professors of history. The Department of Japanese History (*kokushika*) was established in the following year 1889, a few months after the Meiji Constitution was promulgated. This was more than a coincidence: the constitution marked the beginning of a new era but at the same time the new development was based on Japan's own traditions. Shigeno's lecture illustrates this very well.

Work on the official chronological history *Dainihon*

*bennenshi* continued after being transferred to the Imperial University, but the move marked the beginning of the end of official historiography in the tradition of the Six National Histories (*Rikkokushi*) of ancient times. Already, within the former government office, the emphasis had shifted from historiography to the compilation of source materials. This had always been an important feature of the Office, but from 1885 members of the Office travelled extensively around Japan to collect primary sources (*komonjo*) and they continued to do so after 1888. Kume Kunitake, expelled from the Imperial University in 1892, was later to say that he and his colleagues concentrated on the primary sources in order to escape political pressure, but it seems just as likely that, as their work progressed and their sources accumulated, the members of the Office of Historiography realised the impossibility of a definitive history, a *seishi*, because the evidence remains forever incomplete.

Kume's expulsion from the university in 1892 after the publication of his essay '*Shintō wa saiten no kozoku*' (Shinto is a primitive custom of heaven worship) in the magazine *Shikai* is usually regarded as the immediate cause for the closure of the Historiographical Institute the following year. However it was neither the only nor the main cause. As hinted above, there had been dissatisfaction with the *Dainihon bennenshi* for some time. Sino-Japanese (*kanbun*), regarded by some as a dead language, and the slow progress had often been criticised: these were the reasons the education minister Inoue Kowashi (1843–1895) gave when he ordered the closure of the Institute.[13] The year 1893 spelled the end of the *Dainihon bennenshi*, which though nearly completed by then was never published.[14] When the Institute was reopened in 1895 its aim was no longer historiography but the collection and publication of sources, a task the Institute continues to perform to this day.

By 1889 Japan's political leaders did not have to look to the ancient Nara period to find justification for political reforms. The Meiji Restoration was itself beginning to become history and the Meiji Restoration state had started to create its own traditions. In a memorandum in 1889 Shinagawa Yajirō (1843–1900) explained the Meiji Restoration in a way similar to Shigeno Yasutsugu and proposed the compilation of a history of the Restoration.[15] Attempts to compile a definitive history of the Meiji Restoration began around this time resulting in the establishment of the

*Shidankai* Society in 1891. The period preceding the Restoration became a focus of interest, one instance of which is the establishment of the Society for the Inquiry into Old Matters (*kyūji shimonkai*) by historians at the Imperial University, including Shigeno and Kume. The aim of this society was to question former Bakufu official about things which could not be learned from the written sources.[16]

The chronological history *Dainihon hennenshi* was a product of the early Meiji years when the political reformers had to seek justification for their actions in the ancient history of Japan. By the time the constitution was promulgated and the most profound political changes had been completed, the *Dainihon hennenshi* had become antiquated. At the same time the Meiji Restoration had receded into history sufficiently to serve the present in its turn.

## NOTES

1. E.g. Paul Akamatsu *Meiji 1868. Revolution and Counter-Revolution in Japan.* (London: Allen & Unwin 1972).
2. Ferdinand Seibt *Revolution in Europa.* (München: Süddeutscher Verlag, 1979) pp. 23-7, 37.
3. The early history of the *Shiryò hensanjo* is the subject of my Ph.D. dissertation Eine Vergangenheit für die Japanische Nation. Die Entstehung des historischen Forschungsinstituts Tokyò daigaku Shiryò hensanjo (1869-1895) (A Past for the Japanese Nation. The Origin of the Historical Research Institute *Tòkyò daigaku Shiryò hensanjo*), (Verlag Peter Lang, 1992).
4. Sakamoto Tarò *Rikkokushi.* (Yoshikawa kòbunkan 1970).
5. 'Shūshikan fukusòsai Date Munenari-ate fukuchò Shigeno Yasutsugu shokan nitsū' (Two letters from the Vice-Director of the Academy of Historiography Shigeno Yasutsugu to the Vice-President Date Munenari), *Nihon rekishi 507*, 1990 pp. 88-92.
6. *Bo gakushi shiseki hensbu ron: shushikan kaikaku no gi; Sanjòke monjo* (National Diet Library), shorui 55/21.
7. Òkubo Toshiaki 'Meiji kenpò no seitei katei to kokutairon', in *Okubo Toshiaki rekishi chòsakushū 7*, Tokyo. (Yoshikawa kòbunkan). 1988 pp. 291-321; Akimoto Nobuhide 'Taisei kiyò no kenkyū 1-5', in *Shintò gaku 64-8.* 1970/1.
8. *Shushikan kanji Miura Yasushi fosho sòan*, Meiji 13.12; *Iwakura monjo* (National Diet Library) microfilm (dai 6 rui 24). Also in the Imperial Household Archives (*Sankò shiryò zatsusan*, Mei 426, 116). *Itò sangikò bòchoku no Òshū e okuru tuide*, Meiji 15.3.4, *Motoda Eifu monjo* (National Diet Library), 109-15.
9. Shimizu Shin *Meiji kenpò seiteishi 1: Doku Ò ni okeru Itò Hirobumi no kenpò chòsa.* Hara shobò (Meiji hyakunenshi sòsho 165) 1971.

10. Ôkubo Toshiaki (ed.), *Zōtei Shigeno bakushi shigaku ronbunshū* 1, Tokyo. Meichō fukyū kai. 1989 (revised edition; first edition 1938) pp. 286–92.

11. *Bun* 2.6; Shigeno gave a lecture with almost the same content at the Academy of Science (*Tokyō gakushi kaiin*); *Shigeno bakushi shigaku ronbunshū* 1989 pp. 479–92.

12. *Tokyo daigaku hyakunenshi. Shiryō* 1, 1984 pp. 156–8.

13. Kaigo Tokiomi *Inoue Kowashi no kyōiku seisaku.* (Tokyo daigaku shuppan kai). 1968 pp. 1021–2.

14. Manuscript in the *Tokyō daigaku Shiryō hensanjo.*

15. Fujii Kantarō 'Koshishaku Shinagawa Yajirō shi no shūshi iken', *Rekishi chiri* 44.4, 1924 pp. 249–54.

16. Cf. Carol Gluck *Japan's Modern Myths* (Princeton: Princeton University Press, 1985) esp. p. 24.

# 5

# Between revolution and reaction: The Japanese women's movement in the Taisho era

ULRIKE WÖHR

I

FOR HISTORICAL RESEARCH at university level, and not only in Japan, women hardly exist: rarely will one find anything concerning women's history in the renowned historical journals which are, in turn, written by renowned scholars of renowned universities. A notable exception is *Rekishi hyōron*, the March issue of which appears as *Woman's History Special (joseishi tokushū)* every year. Other than that, one usually has to search in the publications of small, local universities and even junior colleges for treatises on women in history. There is, of course, the large number of historical research associations, more or less specialised by field or locality, who encourage and publish research in their sphere, be it family history, the history of Kumamoto or whatever.

There are few exceptions to this rule: women like Fukuda Hideko, Yamakawa Kikue and Ichikawa Fusae have been the subject of research (Ichikawa has herself brought into being one of the most active associations for research on the women's movement, the former Fusen Kaikan, now called Ichikawa Fusae Kaikan, in Tokyo). And perhaps the most dominant in the writings – historical or other – on women in modern Japan are the protagonists of the Seitōsha ('Blue Stocking Society'), the editors and authors of the first literary journal produced by women (*Seitō*, September 1911–February 1916). The names of Hiratsuka Raichō and Itō Noe exist not only in academic and feminist circles but seem, to borrow the words of one Japanese historian, 'like shining stars leading the way for the women's movement'.[1]

Irokawa Daikichi, who wrote this in 1975, goes on to say that almost every book on the history of women in modern

Japan starts with a part on the women of the Seitōsha or by citing Hiratsuka Raichō's so-called 'manifesto' ('*Genshi josei wa taiyō de atta* . . .'). He deems important these women's function as models – which, I may add, is often enforced by idealisation – but speaks up for the replacement of a conception of history that is concerned with the élite only. The greater proportion of Japanese women, he claims, have always belonged to the lower classes, whom even socialist women like Yamakawa Kikue do not really represent.[2]

Irokawa is not saying that personalities like Yamakawa Kikue and Hiratsuka Raichō should not be taken into account by historians, but he demands a broader perspective, a future Women's History, that stresses the following three points:

– Forerunners and leaders of the women's movement (the 'personalities'): how have they made things easier, opened up new possibilities for all women?

– Married women, housewives and mothers: how have they, without being able to escape from the most repressive institution of the whole system, the *ie*, still found ways to liberate themselves?

– Working women: how has their work changed their personalities and attitude? Women working in the licensed quarters, in professions outlawed by society, must also be a subject of Women's History.[3]

Whether or not as a response to this appeal, since the end of the 1970s many historical studies on women's associations of a less glamorous type and of liberationists of only local importance have started to appear. Some of these more recent studies treat phenomena of which Japan's women can be less proud, like the Patriotic Women's Association (Aikoku Fujinkai, established in 1901)[4] and militaristic tendencies[5] among women before and during the Pacific War. Irokawa with his obviously educationalist demand on history may not consider these to be such worthy subjects. There is no doubt, however, that they have shed some light on an unpleasant reality which the Japanese now seem to be prepared to face, whereas in the decades after the war they needed heroines to identify with, to reassure themselves that it had not been all that bad and that there were advocates of liberalism and equal rights before the Americans imposed their democracy on them.

The women's group I am going to consider here, the Shinshin Fujinkai ('True New Women's Society'), rarely appears in historical research about women, despite the increased output of the last decade. One reason for this may be the difficulties in placing this group in a spectrum ranging from the liberal and individualist Seitōsha to the militaristic and Tennō-devoted Aikoku Fujinkai or – even though this may sound polemic – to categorise it as either good or bad.

I cannot hope to rise to the challenge issued by Irokawa in a paper as short as this, but my discussion of the group and the magazine that carries its name will in one way or another involve all three of the points he made. To save this study from being purely descriptive and to help evaluate the phenomenon or at least to provide an idea of its background, allowing one to make comparisons, a contrastive method will be used.

The foil will be the already-mentioned Seitōsha. This is not an arbitrary choice. It is already implied in the name of the group, which deliberately takes up and at the same time criticises the so-called New Woman (*atarashii onna*), embodied in the members of the Seitōsha. Nishikawa Fumiko, one of the founders of the group, has denied ever being resentful of Hiratsuka Raichō and claimed to hold basically the same views as the Seitōsha;[6] however, there is no doubt that Hiratsuka Raichō was resentful of the newcomers and interpreted their very existence as an attack on her group.[7] The press certainly affiliated and compared the two and effectively played them off against one another. And not without some reason: the peg and focus point for all the commentators was the occasion that apparently[8] led the three women, Nishikawa Fumiko, Kimura Komako and Miyazaki Mitsuko, to found a new group.[9]

It took place at the first (and only) open lecture held by the Seitōsha on 15 February 1913. Scheduled to speak, among others, was the naturalist writer and critic Iwano Hōmei, husband of the Seitōsha member Iwano Kiyoko. Hōmei's '*hanju shugi*', a theory implying that man (and woman) had an 'animal side', a part governed by instinct and compulsive desire, that had to be taken into account[10] upset one of the listeners (Miyazaki Toranosuke) so much that he got up and not only reproached Hōmei for his immoral affairs with women but also physically attacked him.[11] Miyazaki was an itinerant preacher, teaching a synchretistic mixture of Buddhism and Christianity and calling himself 'The Prophet'. He was also the husband of Miyazaki

Mitsuko, one of the founders of the Shinshin Fujinkai which came into being shortly after the incident described.

Still the founding of the Shinshin Fujinkai was not just an act of defiance against the Seitōsha, nor is the True New Woman simply a less glamorous imitation of the New Woman. The Shinshin Fujinkai does have an original background and its own roots that are at least as important for the understanding of the Taishō era as the ideas to which Hiratsuka Raichō and other members of the Seitōsha refer. To demonstrate this, I am going to give first the biographies of the three founders. I will then describe the one book that they published as co-authors and their monthly journal *Shinshin Fujin*.

## II

Nishikawa Fumiko,[12] the oldest of the three women, was born in a Gifu-ken village in 1882. Her father was the village headman, a diligent man who had built up quite a fortune during his life. Her mother came from a rather refined family tracing its origins back to one of the generals of Toyotomi Hideyoshi and was, for those days, an unusually educated woman. Both parents were ardent believers of Jōdo Shinshū. Fumiko was born when her mother was 37 years old. The marriage had remained childless for ten years, and most of Fumiko's brothers and sisters died as infants.

Fumiko's school career up to her graduation from higher elementary school was interrupted once for a whole year due to an attack of typhoid fever, the disease that would kill her older sister two years later. Thanks to her oldest brother's support, Fumiko was allowed to go on to higher education at the Kyōto Women's School (*Kyōto-fu jogakkō*). There she made friends with Yosano Akiko's sister, Hō Satoko, who eventually married Fumiko's brother. After finishing the basic five-year course, Fumiko went on to take the supplementary course and, in addition, private English lessons. She also received poetry lessons from Inokuma Natsuki, a traditional man who finally dissuaded her from continuing her studies at the newly founded *Nihon joshi daigaku*.[13]

Something that would eventually change Fumiko's whole life took place in her final year at school. It was a lecture and fund-raising event[14] for the victims of the pollution caused by the Ashio copper mines. The speeches, delivered by Kinoshita Naoe, Tamura Naomi and Ushioda Chiseko, impressed Fumiko so much that she persuaded first her headmaster and then Ushioda Chiseko to have the latter's speech repeated in front of the students of her school.

Even more than that, however, she had been moved by the words of the main organiser of the event, Matsuoka Kōson, then a student at *Dōshisha kōtō gakkō*[15] and a Sunday school teacher at *Rakuyō kyōkai*. When Fumiko called on him after the event, it was the beginning of a very romantic love story. They married nine months later, but not without some difficulties in obtaining her parents' permission – Kōson was, after all, a Christian. He came from an old and still very traditional *bushi* family in Kumamoto-ken. As a poet,[16] he was strongly influenced by nineteenth-century English Romanticism and by the poetry of Kitamura Tōkoku and Shimazaki Tōson; his feelings of compassion for the poor and oppressed were greatly fostered by the Christian socialism of his teacher, Abe Isoo.[17]

By the time of their marriage, Kōson was working in an orphanage in the countryside of Gifu-ken, Fumiko had become a teacher at the Ogaki Higher Girls School and was living at her parents' house. After marrying, they at first both continued working, but Fumiko was soon fired for fear that, with her 'free love marriage',[18] she would set a bad example for the students.

In early 1903 the couple moved to Tōkyō where Kōson was going to enter the preparatory course of Waseda *daigaku*. Kōson became a member[19] of Abe Isoo's Shakai Shugi Kyōkai,[20] and when the Heiminsha[21] was founded, Fumiko often joined him for lectures and the like and, of course, attended the special lecture meetings for women.[22] Meanwhile, Kōson, who had shown signs of suffering from tuberculosis for a long time, declined in strength rapidly, and when summoned to his home town to register for the draft in the wake of the declaration of the Russo-Japanese War, he made the journey to Kyūshū, never to return.[23]

Fumiko was with him in his last moments and returned to Tōkyō three months later to find solace in the close-knit community of the Heiminsha and in her work for its cause. She soon took over household duties in the association's headquarters and also lived there. But she was not one to be satisfied with household chores. At the first Women's Lecture Meeting with women not just as listeners,[24] she was one of the scheduled speakers, and after that continually appeared in front of this audience. She was also one of the few women whose names appear under articles in the

*Heimin Shinbun* and in its successor, *Chokugen*.[25] In early 1905, together with Nobeoka Tameko[26] and a few other women, she launched a petition to the Diet, concerning the revision of Article 5 of the Police Security regulations – the beginning of the Japanese women's long struggle for political rights.

Fumiko's marriage to Nishikawa Kōjirō, then one of the foremost members of the Heiminsha, in February 1905 again changed her life considerably. During the first years of their marriage,[27] Kōjirō was in and out of jail, and as long as the Heiminsha existed, Fumiko was as active as ever. In November of the same year, she gave birth to her first child, and from then on she only sporadically appears on the scene, such as with a short article in Fukuda Hideko's *Sekai Fujin*[28] and a speech at the Socialist Women's Lecture Meeting.[29] Kōjirō had become a member of the newly founded Japan Socialist Party[30] but after being released in July 1910, after another two years in jail,[31] he announced his breaking away from socialism to turn to a religiously influenced moralism.

It is hard to tell how her husband's conversion affected Fumiko. She did take part in his religious and welfare activities but grew more and more impatient and eager to do something on her own. She already had three children when, on the spur of the moment, she decided to get together with Miyazaki Mitsuko and Kimura Komako, two women she hardly knew, to organise regular lecture meetings for women with only female speakers. It was the beginning of the Shinshin Fujinkai that kept her busy for more than ten years.

Miyazaki Mitsuko's life is poorly documented[32] compared with that of Nishikawa Fumiko. She was born in the town of Yanagikawa, Fukuoka-ken, in 1885 as the daughter of a wealthy ceramics merchant and moneylender. Her mother died when Mitsuko was three years old, and when her father remarried, she was brought up by an aunt who died five years later. Three years later her father died, and Mitsuko, a child of 11, was left without anyone to whom she felt close. She did not get along with the wife of her elder brother who himself led a life of licentious indulgence, quickly wasting the family fortune. In 1901, after finishing compulsory school education, she planned to go on to Atomi Girls' School. Due to bad health and financial difficulties, before long she had to leave.

In her desperate search for something dependable in life, she came upon the writings of a fellow citizen of her hometown, Miyazaki Toranosuke, who called himself the 'Messiah-Buddha' and, as is apparent in the name, taught a conglomeration of Buddhism and Christianity which prophesied an imminent world of peace, unified by himself, the 'Prophet'. Mitsuko not only became an ardent believer of his teachings but also fell in love with the man, who was much older than she was. She followed him to Nagoya, where they got married and soon started out together as itinerant preachers, to spread their faith across the whole country. Even when their daughter was born, Mitsuko still followed her husband, carrying the child around.

In Tökyö they built a centre for their religion,[33] and during that time Mitsuko met Nishikawa Fumiko and Kimura Komako and, before long, decided to join them in the organisation of the above-mentioned lecture meetings.

Kimura Komako,[34] born in 1887, is the youngest of the three women. She was the daughter of the chief clerk of a dealer in fire-fighting pumps, but when she was eight years old, her father lost everything he had to an usurer and had to leave the family to find work in Taiwan. Komako had learnt traditional Japanese dance (*Nihon buyō*) since she was three years old and had played girls' *kabuki* (*chinko shibai*) when she was five. When financial disaster threatened the family's existence, Komako helped out by performing for a small, itinerant theatre which toured the countryside around Kumamoto.

Men seem to have been attracted by Komako's beauty ever since she was fairly young, but when it came to marrying, her poverty and her childhood acting proved to be great obstacles. When one man who had first offered to pay for Komako to go to school suddenly offered her parents money to make her his concubine, she ran away from home and started working as the first telephone operator in Kumamoto. Before long, through the good offices of a friend, she had a new patron – Kimura Bansaku, a wealthy maker of soy sauce – who made it possible for her to study at Kumamoto *jogakkō*.[35] After graduation she could have become a teacher herself, but this seemed to her too petty a profession; she was looking for something more glamorous, something to astonish her parents and the whole of Kumamoto.

She had, for a long time, taken English lessons on her own initiative, and her secret dream was to go to America. She therefore went on to study at the Fukuoka English-Japanese Girl's School,[36] but in the same year she changed to the English department of Aoyama *jogakuin* in Kyōto. Again, she did not feel settled, and when in Tōkyō female actresses were given opportunities for the first time,[37] she made up her mind to try acting. Her patron Kimura, however, upon whom she still depended financially, refused to give his permission. Unluckily, the school authorities had got wind of her ideas, and she was suspended at once. Her next plan was to become a doctor, so she went to study with a female doctor.

In May 1907 Komako's dream of going to America came very close to coming true. A rich friend's uncle was going to pay for the journey, and Kimura had agreed to give her the money to study there. But when everything was settled, Komako refused to go. This time love was the reason for her unexpected decision, and it was a double setback for her patron Kimura, as the chosen object happened to be his nephew and heir, Kimura Hideo, whom he had intended to marry off well. Hideo was disowned, and Komako was turned out of her parents' house. They were shunned by Kumamoto society, but they lived together unconcerned about their reputation, carried away by their love and by their religious fervour.

Hideo had – from his student days at Dōshisha[38] – been interested in religion and this was one of the reasons why his uncle sent him to study in America, in the hope that he would return a little more business-minded. However, at Berkeley Hideo chose Religious Studies as his subject and concerned himself mainly with Indian Tantrism. Back in Japan, he founded the Japanese Association for Spiritual Research[39] and taught techniques of hypnosis. Komako became his first adherent, and later published a book on their new religion.[40]

During their time in Kumamoto, for about four months Komako was an active contributor to *Kumamoto byōron*,[41] the only journal of the socialist movement in the whole of Kyūshū. Her name does not appear after January 1908 for one, because she became an (illegitimate!) mother in February, and also because the police had started to keep an eye on her. Not that her contributions to *Kumamoto byōron* were exactly socialist; they were more of an outcry for the liberation of thought, in an individual rather than in a political sense, and for a 'revolution' of the arts, namely the theatre.[42] But the use of the word '*kakumei*' was enough of an offence to have her registered as 'developing into a socialist'.[43]

Komako, as can be seen, had not lost her interest in the theatre and was, in fact, still dreaming of becoming an actress. Their severe financial problems also made it seem reasonable for Komako to take up a profession, so she applied to the Imperial Actresses Training School[44] which had just opened its doors. Of the 15 women who were accepted, she was the only one not from Tōkyō, but when it was discovered that she had a baby, the school withdrew its permission. There was no stopping her, however; in May 1909 the three of them left Kumamoto, where social pressure had become almost unbearable, and in autumn they opened a treatment centre in Tōkyō, using Hideo's techniques of hypnosis for healing.

In the autumn of 1911 Komako, by now the mother of two children and legally married, succeeded in obtaining a place at the practical arts school that was the successor of the Imperial Actresses Training School,[45] and began a new attempt at acting. Unlike most of her fellow students who came from rich families, she understood acting to be means to make a living, and soon became dissatisfied with the school. She left after her one-year-old daughter died in the summer of 1912.

Towards the end of the same year, she got to know Nishikawa Fumiko and Miyazaki Mitsuko, with whom she planned to organise women's lecture meetings, the first of which was to take place in June 1913.

The striking differences between the three women in background as well as in character had already been noticed by their contemporaries, for instance, by Hiratsuka Raichō who, at a time when the names of Miyazaki Mitsuko and Kimura Komako had already vanished from the table of contents of the journal *Shinshin Fujin*, claimed to have presumed from the start that such a heterogeneous group would not exist for long.[46] However, especially in contrast to Hiratsuka Raichō's Seitōsha, the three women do have some important points in common. The contemporary journalist Yoshino Gajō points out the differences between the two groups' protagonists with a sure eye.[47]

One difference he notes was probably even more

important then than it is now:[48] none of the three founders of the Shinshin Fujinkai are from Tōkyō, unlike most of the women of the Seitōsha. This, he supposes, accounts for the passion and the spirituality that clearly distinguishes them from the lucid emotionality and the feeling for art of the Tōkyō women.[49]

Another point Yoshino makes is the three women's status as wives and mothers. This implies a way of life differing greatly from the rather carefree existence of the young ladies of the Seitōsha. As one more consequence of their being married, he mentions the influence undoubtedly exerted on them by their husbands, all of whom Yoshino considers to be religious or moral agitators.[50] This opinion can certainly be questioned, especially in the case of Nishikawa Fumiko and Kimura Komako, but the conspicuousness of Miyazaki Toranosuke at the Seitōsha event and at the first of the Shinshin Fujinkai's lecture meetings certainly helped to start a rumour. There is no reason, however, why Seitōsha members should not have been influenced by men who did not happen to be their husbands. Even Yoshino remarks on the ambition of the Shinshin Fujinkai to feature only female speakers, in contrast to the Seitōsha,[51] and as the first version of their *Manifesto* shows, they prided themselves on publishing their journal 'without depending on any direct help from men'.[52]

More important perhaps than the actual influence of their husbands is the fact of their having to cope with a family. As a result of their own experience of the difficulty of asserting themselves as personalities in the midst of household duties, they try to reach this same kind of woman in the audience. To quote their *Manifesto* again: '. . . we encourage women who are housewives already, not to sink into passive self-destruction and self-abandonment, but to persist actively . . .'.[53] This aim offers quite a contrast to the Seitō women's objectives to liberate themselves by the means of a literary magazine which 'absolutely has to be a magazine for our own sake'[54] and to Hiratsuka Raichō's outcry, 'I hate all the trouble of housework, as it will hinder the development of hidden talents . . .'.[55]

This leads to another very obvious difference between the two groups, which also derives from the differences in their founders' life histories. Unlike the Seitōsha which, as can be seen, did not feel obliged to free and enlighten Japanese women in general and hardly recognised the 'woman question' (*fujin mondai*) 'as a social question',[56] the members of the Shinshin Fujinkai not only raised issues like women's education, working women, social pressure on women etc. but also concerned themselves with educational and welfare work. Apart from their regular lecture meetings, they organised lectures and a street campaign to draw attention to and collect money for the victims of the famine in Tōhoku and Hokkaidō,[57] and they opened a counselling centre which not only offered marriage counselling but also gave vocational guidance and tried to find jobs for women.[58] They considered themselves to be part of a movement on not just a national but a worldwide scale,[59] and this certainly has roots in their universalism, inspired by religion and socialism. This attitude may account for the generosity – at least by Nishikawa Fumiko – to include the presumed opponent Seitōsha in the imaginary movement.[60]

And in some respects, the True New Women are not that different from the New Women. None of them questions marriage itself – how could they, as they all are married – but they are advocates of 'free love' (*jiyū ren'ai*) and of a 'free love marriage' (*jiyū ren'ai kekkon*) which all three of them have experienced themselves and which – at least for Nishikawa Fumiko who had to give up teaching and for Kimura Komako who was discriminated against in her community – meant great disadvantages and harassment. The Seitōsha women, even though not all of them are as consistent as Hiratsuka Raichō, usually take up a critical stance on the institution of marriage as part of the repressive *ie*-system.[61] At this point, it seems necessary to note the difference in age between the protagonists of the two groups: there is a difference of only four years between Nishikawa Fumiko and Hiratsuka Raichō, but many of the Seitōsha members were ten or more years younger than the former,[62] which in such fast-moving times must have almost presented a generation gap. And Hiratsuka Raichō, who liked to stress the fact of the Seitōsha women's youth,[63] witnessed the resignation of many members from the group, as a consequence of their marriage.[64]

### III

Among the common experiences of the Shinshin Fujinkai's three founders, 'free love' may have been the strongest bond. But, as the table of contents of their journal shows, their alliance was rather short-lived: Kimura Komako's last contribution, a review of Hiratsuka Raichò's book *Maru mado yon*,[65] was published in the fourth issue, in August 1913, and the last news from Miyazaki Mitsuko, consisting of a letter from Osaka,[66] appeared in the same issue. There is no hint as to why the two women stopped contributing, either in the journal's column 'From the Editorial Office' or in any of the biographical sources. Miyazaki Mitsuko, as she writes in her letter, had gone off with her husband, to spread their religion outside of Tòkyò, but of Kimura Komako we only know that in February 1914 she gave birth to another daughter whom she also lost as a baby, and that from the end of 1914, she finally realised her dream to become an actress, at a theatre in Asakusa.[67]

Whatever the reasons for their splitting up – that there may have been causes for conflict is apparent even in their first co-production, a book with the title *The path for the new woman to take* (i.e. 'Teachings for the new woman')[68] that has been described as a kind of manifesto of the new group.[69] To call this book a co-production is perhaps an overstatement. The three women used it rather as a platform to state – in entirely separate sections – their differing views on what the (True) New Woman should be like and how society and humankind must change and will be changed.

Nishikawa Fumiko's writing is probably the most logically thought out and the easiest to follow. Her argumentation revolves around the seemingly opposing concepts of *ryòsai kenbo* (Good Wife and Wise Mother) and *atarashii onna* (New Woman). She tries to show that they are not really incompatible at all. The (True) New Woman, she states, is not the man-eating and *saké*-gulping creature dragged into the limelight by the press. It is instead a kind of woman that has always existed, with her own, individual idea of how to live her life.[70] The old concept of *ryòsai kenbo* has not lost its validity for the present, it has simply been misunderstood. Being 'good wives' does not mean that they should be their husbands' slaves, and 'good mothers' are not meant to be slaves of the household; indeed, if they are held as slaves, they cannot possibly be good wives or good mothers.[71]

One of the evils leading to intellectual inferiority of women is their own passivity, their own lack of thirst for knowledge which in turn is the result of the traditional division of labour, requiring women to study only to be fit for the practical requirements of the household.[72] Nishikawa calls upon men to accept women as their partners and intellectual equals and harshly criticises those who out-wardly like to discuss the 'woman question' but at home lord over their wives.[73] She does not suggest however, that men alleviate their wives' burden by lending a helping hand in the house. Even though she does hold society's[74] and men's rigid traditional views responsible for many of the problems women are facing, much of her criticism concerns the women themselves – students who use their money on make-up instead of books,[75] girls who marry someone only because he is rich[76] and women who lack the will to develop their intellectual powers.[77] Her suggested method to change the status quo is to form and mobilise women's circles all over the country, to facilitate an exchange of ideas and to enable women to widen their horizons.[78] How she intends to educate women who cannot spare the time to educate themselves remains a mystery.

For Miyazaki Mitsuko, the so-called 'woman question' is the fundamental problem of humankind.[79] Before it can be solved, one basic issue concerning men and women must be settled: are they the same or are they different?[80] Miyazaki's objective at this point is to criticise socialism, which argues from an exclusively materialistic viewpoint,[81] and denies the differences – not only physical but also psychological – between men and women and therefore does not hold marriage and the family in high esteem.[82] For her, the destruction of the family means the destruction of humankind, its return to animal patterns of behaviour.[83] Man and woman alone are incomplete – they complement each other to make a full human being.[84] That they are different must be taken into account when speaking of equal chances and equal payment of work: women in jobs demanding physical strength, cannot possibly do the same amount of work as men. For such cases, Miyazaki suggests equal payment on a time basis.[85]

According to her, the special qualities of women will become apparent once they have taken over public positions in society, and she presents a whole array of examples from 'women in parliament' to 'women in the economic world'. To emphasise the good effects of their participation, she often cites Western examples.[86] For these reasons, she is an ardent advocate of women's suffrage, but she criticises any use of violence or of vulgar acts such as seen among the English suffragettes.[87] Instead, she believes in the laws of evolution, according to which humanity will naturally develop for the better.[88] Faith is the path that will eventually take humanity to its perfection, and Miyazaki therefore laments the alleged lack of religious interest of the Japanese in her day.[89]

The part contributed by Kimura Komako is the most contradictory and confusing even though its outward structure – the six steps of woman's spiritual development to her highest perfection – makes it seem the most organised. The New Woman which is ridiculed by the press is a product of its time and by nature a contradictory creature. Having been granted access to intellectual spheres for only a few decades, she now has the status of an intelligent cripple.[90] Not content with this, she will develop along the following lines: the first step, intellectual vanity (as opposed to the materialistic vanity of the 'old woman') will, secondly, lead to a deep fall. At some point, she will re-emerge from the depths of her dissolute life to search for the true life, for self-awareness (*jikaku*). For a woman the achievement of *jikaku* is invariably connected with love, as love is the driving force in a woman.[91] Self-awareness will make her realise woman's true nature, and she will hence voluntarily obey the rules of chastity and fidelity and look for a man to subjugate her.[92]

Kimura goes on to speaking about woman's still hidden talent, which repeated practice will bring out, and about her original thinking, both of which are apparent especially in art.[93] More strenuous effort will take woman to the realm of *kanjizai*, described as 'free imagination'. The last chapter, called 'The Inner Life of a Mystic' (meaning herself), elaborates on this idea which, as may have been guessed, is the basic concept of Kimura Hideo's New Religion.

Even though there are similarities in the three women's ideas and in their ways of arguing a point, there are a few crucial elements which may have caused them to fall out with one another. Possibly the most important is Miyazaki's strong resentment against socialism (and also against naturalism), basically motivated by her rejection of materialism. This implies her minimising the contribution of economic and social factors in the development and progress of mankind – her evolution is a purely spiritual one. It also causes her to deny any influence of physical instincts or sexual desire on people's ways of acting and reacting. Her denial of the importance of economic and social factors obviously conflicts with the views of Nishikawa, who laments the social and educational discrimination of women and, similar to socialism, sees its cause in the division of labour. Miyazaki's refusal to acknowledge instinct and desire as considerable forces marks a contrast to Kimura, who does acknowledge them, even though in her eyes they characterise a stage in a woman's development which must and will be overcome.

The other possible source of conflict I want to mention may have been their differing religious convictions. Miyazaki's and Kimura's were particularly strong and run through the whole of their respective arguments.[94] Miyazaki, at the end of her part of the book, establishes the prophets' (and the present and most important one, of course, her husband's) duty and vocation to lead people – and here especially women – to self-awareness (jikaku).[95] This implies a claim to the leadership of her religion to which Kimura may not have wanted to submit.

One issue that would have been very interesting – but also rather lengthy – to discuss is the varying connotations of the central term 'jikaku' within the three founders' writings as well as compared with its meaning(s) in the Seitō. Whoever first coined the term, it has been used for a whole array of different concepts. Such meta-discussions were never an issue then, and it seems that there was no awareness of the different usages of jikaku among the founders of one women's group, certainly not enough to be held responsible for the splitting of the three women.

IV

To conclude this short and therefore superficial study of the Shinshin Fujinkai, I would like to give some idea of the appearance and contents of their journal Shinshin Fujin which appeared from May 1913 to September 1923. Here, once more, the Seitōsha with its journal Seitō presents itself as a yardstick of comparison.

A severe drawback for the study of Shinshin Fujinkai is the disastrous situation concerning the main source material: only the first two volumes of the journal are complete (24 issues, May 1913 to April 1915).[96] Another 14 single copies of the original 24 issues can be found in libraries and in private ownership.[97] Very regrettable is the fact that a relatively recent publication of otherwise great bibliographical value, a collection of tables of contents of about 30 different women's magazines appearing from 1884 to 1945

(*Kindai fujin zasshi mokuji sòran*[98]), does not include the Shinshin Fujin, even though its editors claim to have concentrated on material particularly difficult to obtain.[99]

Given the circumstances described above and also the fact that my entire discussion up to now has concentrated on the Shinshin Fujinkai at an early stage of its existence, I shall base what I am going to say about the journal on the first volume (May 1913 to April 1914). Unfortunately, I have not yet obtained information on its circulation size at any time, but the fact that so few copies have survived may indicate a rather small print run.

The contemporary informant, Yoshino Gajô, who has previously been cited, describes it as 'extremely meagre by comparison with the *Seitō*, . . . without any splendour'.[100] The 52 pages of its first issue (expanding to little more than 60 pages towards the end of the first volume) are indeed meagre when compared with the sometimes more than 200 pages of the *Seitō* at that time.[101] Its closely spaced lines and densely printed succession of articles, leaving no space for illustrations, does make the *Shinshin Fujin* a very poor sibling of the *Seitō* and hints at the difference in the economic backgrounds of the respective founders. Another reason why the journal's pages look so packed are the *furigana*[102] printed at the side of every single Chinese character as a reading-aid. The *Seitō* lacks *furigana*, but all the socialist journals with which Nishikawa Fumiko was familiar[103] had them. The implication is that the *Shinshin Fujin* was obviously aiming at readers who were not necessarily well educated, whereas the *Seitō* would not have given such people much of a chance.

But what kind of texts does this journal contain, and who are the authors? A first look at the tables of contents shows quite a number of familiar names: Sōma Kokkō,[104] Oguchi Michiko,[105] Sōma Gyofū,[106] Tsukahara Jūshien,[107] Takashima Beihō,[108] Tamura Toshiko,[109] Yamaji Aizan,[110] Yosano Akiko,[111] Takayasu Gekkō[112] and Yoshioka Yayoi,[113] to name only a few. Some of them appear only as subjects of interviews reported in the journal, but most of them make one and usually more contributions. Some of the names, such as those of Yosano Akiko and Tamura Toshiko, more often appear in the *Seitō*, especially in the early years. The others did not have such an intermediate position, but they certainly were intellectual figures of the time.[114] It is noteworthy that the socialist and anarchist scene is not represented, but one should be aware that people like Yamakawa Kikue were very critical of both the Shinshin Fujinkai and the Seitōsha.[115]

But where are the women who were supposed to be educated? Besides the contributions of the three founders and of Oguchi Michiko, there are the stories of a woman called Toribayashi Aguri[116] which Yoshino, rather cynically, judges to be 'not bad for housewives' art'.[117] Other than that, there is a prize contest for *haiku* and *tanka*, the best of which appear on the final pages of every issue. Interestingly enough, the journal did start out with a contest for – among other things, like sketches and poems – 'essays on women's issues'[118] but dropped this after the third issue. The *Shinshin Fujin* was, after all, not a journal made by women 'for their own sake' but for the education of other women who, in consequence, were confined to the readership.

Of course, the *Shinshin Fujin* lacks the *Seitō*'s literary sophistication, as this is not what its editors stressed. They did, however, make an effort to introduce foreign literature. One example is the translation of a story by Chekov,[119] done by Senuma Kayō[120] who had been translating Chekov and other Russian and Polish authors in the *Seitō*. Another interesting example is the discussion of G.B. Shaw's play *Candida*,[121] the story of a woman who has to decide between her husband and a young man who desires her and who finally decides in favour of her husband without thereby losing her inner independence. *Candida* has been called 'Shaw's answer to Ibsen's *Nora*',[122] and it is hardly a coincidence that the True New Women felt attracted to this 'madonna of common sense',[123] two years after the New Women's discussion of *Nora*.[124]

Women's issues and the discussion of the 'woman question', had from the start, been the main objective of the journal, and the articles relating to these subjects usually have a didactic note. There is, for instance, the presentation of Olive Schreiner's book, *Woman and Labour*,[125] which is mostly a literal translation, heavily annotated by the translator, but in some parts takes the form of a discussion of Schreiner's ideas, interrupted by quotations from her work. This complies with the aims of the Shinshin Fujinkai to 'take the best of what is published in journals of the European and American women's movement and always try to explain . . .',[126] but it is strikingly different from the *Seitō*'s way of presenting foreign feminist literature: here the

66

translations lack any annotations, and their contents are usually not discussed in the journal.[127]

## V

I would like to close without anything resembling a final evaluation of the group or of its journal, leaving that to a more in-depth study. I think it has been made clear, that they form an important piece in the jigsaw of the discussion of the 'woman question' in the Taishō era. According to another famous Japanese historian, Kano Masanao, Woman's History teaches that 'Man's History should be taken for what it is, instead of considering it to be the equivalent of History as such'.[128] The history of a group like the Shinshin Fujinkai may teach us not to take the Seitōsha's history to be Woman's History as such.

## NOTES

1. Irokawa Daikichi. "Fujin kòron" ga ayunda rokujūnen to joseitachi (tokubetsu kikaku)', Koshò Yukiko (ed.), *Joseishi ronsò*. Tòkyò: Domesu shuppan, 1987 pp. 32–4. (Abridged version of an article first published in *Fujin kòron*, Vol. 60, No. 6, 1975).
2. *Ibid.*, p. 33.
3. *Ibid.*, p. 33f.
4. E.g. Nagahara Kazuko. 'Aikoku fujinkai no katsudò. Josei kokka, sensò kyòiku wo megutte', *Rekishi byòron* 49 (1979), pp. 177–22. And Saji Emiko. 'Gunji engo to katei fujin. Shoki fujin. Shoki aikoku fujinkai ron', Kindai joseishi kenkyūkai (ed.), *Onnatachi no kindai*. Tòkyò: Kashiwa shobò, 1978. pp. 116–43.
5. E.g. Nishikawa Yūko. 'Sensò e no keisha to uyoku no fujin', Joseishi sògò kenkyūkai (ed.), *Nihon joseishi* Vol. 5. Tòkyò: (Tòkyò daigaku shuppankai, 1982) pp. 227–63.
6. As she stated in her autobiography: Amano Shigeru (ed.): *Heiminsha no onna. Nishikawa Fumiko jiden*. (Tòkyò: Aoyama kan, 1984) p. 134f.
7. Hiratsuka Raichò: Nishikawa Fumiko-shi no "Fujin kaihò ron" wo hyòsu', *Seitò* IV, 5 (March 1914), 22. This review of Nishikawa's book is, as she states herself, the first time that she comments on the Shinshin Fujinkai at all and so publicly acknowledges its existence.
8. Miyazaki Mitsuko in *Tòkyò Nichi Nichi Shinbun*, 1 March 1913 (quoted by Amano Shigeru (ed.) *Heiminsha no onna. Nishikawa Fumiko jiden*. Tòkyò: Aoyama kan, 1984. 348f).
9. To organise regular lecture meetings for women had, however, been a plan that the women had thought up between the three of them much earlier. (Amano 1984 p. 118f.; Ishihara Michiko: 'Kimura Komako, "Kumamoto hyòron" no onna', in the same author's book *'Kumamoto byòron' no onna*. (Tòkyò/Kumamoto: Kazokushi kenkyūkai, 1989) p. 26.)
10. Iwano Hòmei: 'Danshi kara suru yòkyò', *Seitò* III, 3 (March 1913) pp. 8–32 (appendix).
11. Tekkenzen (pseudonym of Yoshino Gajò): 'Shinshin Fujinkai no

naimen kansatsu', *Chūō kōron* (rinji sōkan fujin mondai go) 1 July 1913, p. 13.

12. All the information concerning Nishikawa Fumiko's biography is taken from her autobiography (note 6).

13. Japan Women's University, founded in 1901 by the Christian educationalist Naruse Jinzō (1858–1919), with the traditionalist ideal of making out of young women 'good wives and wise mothers' (*ryōsai kenbo*).

14. Held on 7 February 1902 at the Rakuyō kyōkai in Kyōto.

15. Dōshisha was founded in 1875 under the name of Dōshisha eigakkō (D. English School) by Niijima Jō who had illegally left Japan during the final years of the Edo period and had come back as a Christian theologian and missionary in 1874.

16. His writings, including what was hitherto unpublished, were edited and published after his death under the title of *Kōson ikō*. Tōkyō: Kokkōsha, 1905 (Facsimile: Tōkyō: Fuji shuppan, 1982).

17. (1865–1949); then Vice Principal of the Dōshisha middle school (refer also to note 20).

18. *Jiyū ren'ai kekkon*.

19. Fumiko could not possibly have become a member, as Article 5 of the Police Security regulations (*chian keisatsubō*) banned women from joining political associations.

20. 'Socialist Association', in existence from January 1900 to November 1904, successor of Shakai shugi kenkyūkai ('Association for the Research of Socialism'); the core of the early socialist movement, from the beginning a group of about 40, with Katayama Sen, Nishikawa Kōjirō, Kōtoku Shūsui, Kinoshita Naoe among the members and Abe Isoo as chairman.

21. 'Commoners' Association', founded in November 1903 by Kōtoku Shūsui and Sakai Toshihiko, very soon almost identical to Shakai shugi kyōkai, in locality as well as in membership; its journal *Heimin shinbun* ('Commoners' News') was published until January 1905 and followed by *Chokugen* ('Plain Talk') which was ordered to suspend publication in September 1905. The Heiminsha, divided by disagreement, disbanded shortly afterwards.

22. *Shakai shugi fujin enzetsukai*, held for the first time on 23 January 1904, was organised monthly by the Heiminsha which also provided most of the (male!) speakers.

23. He died at the age of 25 on 23 July 1904.

24. Seemingly, the meetings had, from the beginning, been organised by women who then 'found themselves crowded out of their own meetings by men who came to hear the male speakers they had scheduled', so that they ended up making it compulsory for every man to be accompanied by a woman. [Sharon L. Sievers: *Flowers in Salt. The Beginnings of Feminist Consciousness in Modern Japan*. (Stanford, Cal.: Stanford University Press, 1983) p. 120.]

25. According to Sievers (note 24), 'it is difficult to determine whether women writers contributed in a significant way . . ., owing to the liberal use of pen names and the prevalence of unsigned articles' (p. 122).

26. She later married Sakai Toshihiko.

27. The actual ceremony took place in September, when Kōjirō was out of jail, but they 'entered a married life' before he went to jail (together with

Kōtoku Shūsui, on 28 February 1905).

28. E.g. 'Onna no kōfuku', *Sekai fujin* No. 37 (5.6.1909), as stated by Amano 1934 p. 403 (note 6). *Sekai fujin* ('Women of the World') was founded by Fukuda Hideko in January 1907 and in 38 issues appeared until July 1909, with the objective to give information on the 'woman question'. On the title page, men were also addressed as part of the readership.

29. Amano 1984 p. 404 (note 6). The *Shakaishugi fujin enzetsukai* was continued even after the Heiminsha's dissolution, proving the relative independence of the women's efforts from the men's factional strifes.

30. Nihon shakaitō, first legal Socialist Party in Japan, founded on 28 January 1906, after the group around Nishikawa Kōjirō, taking advantage of the less restrictive policy of the new prime minister Saionji Kinmochi, had founded the Nihon heimintō (14 January). The two parties fused on 24 February of the same year.

31. By this time the high treason incident (*taigyaku jiken*) at the end of which Kōtoku Shūsui and 23 other leading socialists (among them one women, Kanno Suga) would be sentenced to death and killed, was already in progress, and Nishikawa was paradoxically saved by his imprisonment.

32. The information concerning Mitsuko's biography is taken from Ishihara Michiko: 'Nishikawa Fumiko, Kimura Komako, Miyazaki Mitsuko cho "Atarashiki onna no iku beki michi" kaisetsu', Nishikawa/Kimura/ Miyazaki: *Atarashiki onna no iku beki michi*. (Facsimile) Tōkyō: Fuji shuppan, 1986 ( = Sōsho 'Seitō' no onnatachi. 15) 1–13 (appendix). Her writings and sermons were published 17 years after her death and provided with an appendix of obituaries of, among many others, 'Hasegawa Shigure, Nishikawa Fumiko, Takashima Beihō, Ikuta Chōkō, Sōma Gyofū. (Kawai Kōshin (ed.): *Mitsuko no koe, so na ta*. Tōkyō: Nakamura Yūraku, 1933.)

33. Shinsei kyōdan.

34. My only source for the following information on her life was Ishihara 1989 pp. 1–46 (note 9).

35. Another Christian-oriented girls' educational institution with the aim of producing 'good wives and wise mothers' (refer to note 13).

36. Fukuoka eiwa jogakkō, founded by an American methodist.

37. One milestone in this development is the founding of Bungei kyōkai (Shimamura Hōgetsu, Tsubouchi Shōyō) in 1906, which endeavoured to create a 'new theatre' (*shin geki*) for Japan and eventually saw that they were not getting anywhere with men in the roles of women. Their first famous actress was Matsui Sumako (1886–1919).

38. When he was a good friend of Matsuoka Kōson.

39. Nihon shinrei kenkyūkai.

40. *Kanji zaijutsu*. (Further details on the book are unknown to me at this point.)

41. Appeared June 1907–September 1908; two men of its staff, Matsuo Uitta (1879–1911) and Niimi Uichirō, were killed in the high treason incident (refer to note 31).

42. The title of her first contribution (*K. byōron*, No. 5, 5 November 1907) was 'Kakumeigeki wo sōshō su' ('Plea for a revolutionary theatre') and was taken by the authorities not as 'a revolution of theatre', but in the sense of 'the theatre of revolution'.

43. In the documents of the Naimushō keihokyoku (the department of the

Ministry of Home Affairs that coordinated the activities of the Secret Police), she is registered with the remark '*shakai shugisha enkaku*' (reg. No. 169).

44. Teikoku joyù yòseijò, founded in 1908 by Kawakami Otojirò (1864–1911) and his wife, the actress Kawakami Sadayakko (1872–1946), with the support of the Imperial Theatre (Teikoku gekijò); the school helped greatly in establishing acting as a somewhat respected and, above all, glamorous profession for women.
45. Teikoku gekijò fuzoku gigei gakkò, established in September 1911.
46. Hiratsuka 1914 p. 22 (note 7).
47. Tekkenzen (pseudonym of Yoshino Gajò): 'Shinshin fujinkai no naimen kansatsu', *Chùò kòron* (rinji sòkan fujin mondaigo), 1 July 1913, pp. 113–20.
48. Refer to Edward Seidensticker: *Low City, High City: Tokyò from Edo to the Earthquake* (Rutland (Vt)/Tòkyò: Tuttle, 1984) and Smith, Henry D. 'Tòkyò as an Idea: An Exploration of Japanese Urban Thought until 1945', *Journal of Japanese Studies* 4, 1 (1978) pp. 45–80.
49. Tekkenzen 1913 p. 117f. (note 47).
50. *Ibid.*, p. 113.
51. *Ibid.*, p. 119.
52. 'Sengen', *Shinshin Fujin*, No. 1 (May 1913), 1. The 'manifesto' was slightly changed from June 1913, and the quoted paragraph was omitted – according to Amano because Nishikawa Fumiko had got her husband to help her with editing (Amano 1984 p. 363; refer to note 6).
53. 'Sengen', *Shinshin Fujin* No. 1 (May 1913), 1.
54. 'Henshùshitsu yori', *Seitò* I, 1 (September 1911), p. 134.
55. Hiratsuka Raichò: 'Genshi josei wa taiyò de atta. Seitò hakkan ni saishite'. *Seitò* I, 1 (September 1991), p. 42.
56. See Hiratsuka on the 'misunderstood' women's liberation that sees its fulfilment in social and political freedom . . . (Hiratsuka 1911 p. p. 47; note 56). One of the exceptions among the Seitòsha members is Katò Midori who was greatly concerned with political and economical issues. (Margret Neuss '*Die Seitòsha. Der Ausgangspunkt der japanischen Frauenbewegung in seinen zeitgeschichtlichen und sozialen Bedingungen*', *Oriens extremus*, XVIII (1971), p. 38.)
57. 'Tòhoku kyùmin no tame ni', *Shinshin Fujin* No. 10 (February 1914),
45. 'Robò katsudò no ki', *Shinshin Fujin* No. 11 (March 1914), 6–17. 'Kyùzaikin boshù kessan hòkoku', *Shinshin Fujin* No. 11 (March 1914), 18.
58. 'Honsha no sòdanbù', *Shinshin Fujin* No. 9 (January 1914), 12.
59. Their 'Manifesto' contains an appeal to 'our sisters in the whole world' with the plea for spiritual support ('Sengen', *Shinshin Fujin* No. 1 (May 1913), 1).
60. Amano 1984 p. 135 (note 6).
61. Neuss 1971 p. 36f. (note 56).
62. Itò Noe: 13 years, Odake Kòkichi: 11 years, Iwano Kiyo: 10 years.
63. Hiratsuka 1911 p. 53 (note 55).
64. Neuss 1971 p. 40 (note 56).
65. *Shinshin Fujin* No. 4 (August 1913), pp. 41–2.
66. *Ibid.*, p. 47.
67. Ishihara 1989, p. 35f. (note 9).
68. Nishikawa Fumiko, Kimura Komako and Miyazaki Mitsuko: *Atarashiki*

*onna no iku beki michi*. Tòkyò: Rakuyòdò April 1913.
69. Ishihara 1986 p. 1 (note 32).
70. Nishikawa/Kimura/Miyazaki 1913 p. 25f. (note 68).
71. *Ibid.*, p. 26f.
72. *Ibid.*, p. 81f.
73. *Ibid.*, p. 72ff.
74. *Ibid.*, p. 83ff.
75. *Ibid.*, p. 3.
76. *Ibid.*, p. 34f.
77. *Ibid.*, p. 7.
78. *Ibid.*, p. 11ff.
79. *Ibid.*, p. 163.
80. *Ibid.*, p. 174f.
81. Also the reason for her anger at (literary) naturalism (*Ibid.*, p. 210).
82. *Ibid.*, p. 169ff.
83. *Ibid.*, p. 196ff.
84. *Ibid.*, p. 206.
85. *Ibid.*, p. 191f.
86. *Ibid.*, p. 181ff.
87. *Ibid.*, p. 182f.
88. *Ibid.*, p. 202.
89. *Ibid.*, p. 237ff.
90. *Ibid.*, p. 91ff.
91. *Ibid.*, p. 96ff.
92. *Ibid.*, p. 112.
93. *Ibid.*, p. 114ff.
94. Nishikawa Fumiko seems to have been affiliated, together with her husband, to Matsumura Kaiseki's 'Michi no kai' (founded in 1908 under the name of 'Nihon kyòkai') which taught a basically Christian religion, Japanised by Buddhist elements. Her involvement and conviction, however, never seem to have been strong enough to influence her way of arguing on the 'women question'. (Amano 1984 p. 110f.; refer to note 6).
95. Nishikawa/Kimura/Miyazaki 1913, p. 251 (note 68).
96. In possession of Amano Shigeru, Kòbe.
97. Refer to Amano 1984 p. 363 (note 6) for detailed information.
98. 15 vols. Ed. by Kindai josei bunkashi kenkyùkai. Tòkyò: òzorasha, 1985–6.
99. ' "Kindai fujin zasshi mokuji sòran" no kanshù ni atatte, *Kindai fujin zasshi mokuji sòran*', Vol. 1, 2nd page (without page No.) (note 98).
100. Tekkenzen 1913 p. 120 (note 47).
101. The *Seitò* had started out with 134 pages in September 1911.
102. Phonetic transcription of Chinese ideographs (*kanji*), given in the letters of the Japanese phonetic syllabary (*kana*) at the side of the respective *kanji*.
103. E.g. *Heimin shinbun, Chokugen*, and *Sekai fujin*.
104. (1876–1955) Businesswoman and patron of the arts. Her bakery in Tòkyò functioned as a salon for artists and intellectuals, regardless of their artistic and political views.
105. (1883–?) Originally a school teacher, she later became a cosmetics specialist. She was active in the Heiminsha (maiden name Teramoto), later contributed to the Sakai Toshihiko's magazine *Hechima no hana* and

eventually became a member of the Shinshin Fujinkai.

106. (1883–1950) Poet and critic, a reformer of Japanese poetry under the influence of naturalism, later also a social critic, influenced by Osugi Sakae but arguing largely along the lines of the individualism and humanism of the Shirakabaha.

107. (1848–1917) Starting out as a journalist, he later became an author of mainly political and historical novels.

108. (1875–1949) Buddhist and active social reformer who allied with Christian groups in a movement for the prohibition of alcohol and prostitution.

109. (1884–1945) Novelist, writing in the naturalist vein (*Akirame*, 1911) and affiliated with the Seitōsha.

110. (1864–1917) Journalist and editor of the magazine *Dokuritsu byōron*. He was a Christian, but later in his thought he blended Confucianism and historical materialism, and founded the Kokka shakaitō in 1905.

111. (1878–1942) As a poet, important in the movement for modernisation of Japanese poetry (*Midaregami*, 1901), as a feminist writer, affiliated to the Seitōsha. Her sister Satoko was married to the brother of Nishikawa Fumiko.

112. (1869–1944) Poet, playwright and the first translator of Ibsen's *Nora* into Japanese.

113. (1871–1959) She was a physician and the founder of Japan's first medical college for women (Tōkyō joi gakkō), but also a member of various government and public organisations.

114. Nishikawa Fumiko and Kōjirō had, for many years, been at the centre of the (Christian) socialist intellectual world and had a large circle of friends and acquaintances within and outside socialism who did not necessarily break with them after Kōjirō's *tenkō* (Amano 1984 p. 109f.; refer to note 6).

115. In her biography she criticises both groups (Yamakawa Kikue: *Onna nidai no ki*. Tōkyō: Heibonsha, 1972. p. 153ff.)

116. Pseudonym of Hinata Yoshiko (Tetsu 1913 p. 120; refer to note 47).

117. *Ibid.*

118. *Shinshin Fujin* No. 1 (May 1913), 52.

119. 'Kashitanka' (Kastanka) – appeared in the *Shinshin Fujin*, starting from No. 5 (September 1913). The story is listed in *Meiji, Taishō, Shōwa honyaku bungaku mokuroku* (Tōkyō: Fūkan shobō, 1984) which is compiled by the Kokuritsu kokkai toshokan which from 1912 onwards contains only book publications, as translated into Japanese for the first time by Nakamura Hakuyō in 1922 – another indication of the non-existence of the Shinshin Fujinkai and its journal in the minds of today's scholars.

120. (1875–1915) Brought up in the Russian orthodox faith, she learned Russian from when she was fairly young. She polished her literary skills under the guidance of Ozaki Kōyō and became one of the most important translators of Russian literature in her day.

121. *Shinshin Fujin* No. 10 (February 1914), 60–70. The play had not yet been staged in Japan, so the discussion is probably based on its first translation, done in 1913 by the Bungei kyōkai member Kawatake Shigetoshi (1889–1967).

122. Kienzle/zur Nedden/Ruppel (ed.): *Reclam's Schauspielführer*. 17th edition. Stuttgart: P. Reclam jun., 1986 p. 775.

123. *Ibid.*, p. 775f.
124. *Furoku Nora* (Nora appendix), Seitò II, 1 (January 1912).
125. (1855–1920) South African author and feminist.
126. Amano 1984 p. 137 (note 6).
127. The only exception is Hiratsuka Raichò's introduction to her translation of Ellen Key's 'Ren'ai to kekkon' (*Seitò* III, 1 (January 1913), pp. 1–19 (appendix)).
128. Kano Masanao: 'Aru kansò', Koshò Yukiko (ed.): *Joseishi ronsò* (Tòkyò: Domesu shuppan, 1987) 35. (First published in *Rekishi byòron*, March 1976).

6

# Green before their time?
# The pre-war Japanese
# anarchist movement[1]

JOHN CRUMP

IN *GREEN POLITICAL THOUGHT*, Andrew Dobson asserts that 'we must understand Green, in a political sense, to be historically specific'.[2] Essentially, what he is arguing is that Green is a political response to the threat of ecological catastrophe which has emerged during only the past couple of decades. Prior to this, Green elements might have occurred in the ideas of this political thinker or that political movement, but a sustained Green critique of existing society and the posing of a consistently Green alternative could not have arisen because the conditions for bringing these about had not yet developed. Hence Dobson maintains that: 'these are obvious ways in which the fully developed ideology of the Green movement could not have existed up to now. It is clear, for instance, that the gloomy future predicted for us would have no persuasive purchase if damage to ecosystems had not reached levels that can sensibly be argued to be globally disruptive.'[3]

Dobson also asserts that to be truly Green not only must the conditions which he sees as allowing this be in existence, but certain key components of Green ideology have to coalesce. These he identifies as 'a description of the limits to growth, the prescription of a fundamental change of political and social direction in response to this description, and the ready availability of the message to a wide audience'.[4] For those not familiar with Green modes of thought, a word of explanation is perhaps required on the expression 'the limits to growth', since this is less transparent than the other necessary components of Green ideology to which Dobson refers. The contention behind 'the limits to growth' is that production in the late twentieth century has reached a level which the planet can no longer sustain for a number of interconnected reasons, such as the depletion of resources and pollution. Faced with the recognition that the limits of sustainable economic activity have now been exceeded, Greens respond by posing 'the sustainable society' as an alternative. Green politics then boils down to theorising the social, political and economic arrangements which 'the sustainable society' would entail, propagandising its desirability and/or necessity, and organising to bring it about.

In this paper I shall challenge the view of those like Dobson that Green is specific to the historical period which commenced in the1970s. I hope to demonstrate that the 'pure anarchist' ( 純正無政府主義 /junsei museifushugi) wing of the Japanese anarchist movement of the 1920s and 1930s struggled to achieve a society which, had it come about, would have been immeasurably Greener than the path towards industrialisation, urbanisation, militarism and imperialism that Japanese capitalism actually took. It is true that the 'pure anarchists' used an entirely different vocabulary to that employed by modern Greens. Rather than 'ecologism', they campaigned for 'anarchist communism'. Instead of 'politics for life', they wanted a 'life without politics'. Yet the alternative society to which these verbal formulae referred was one which would have met certainly most, and perhaps all, of the criteria demanded by modern Greens (deindustrialisation, deurbanisation, decentralisation, reassessment of consumption, etc.). Furthermore, in certain important respects, the 'pure anarchists' did not flinch from drawing Greener conclusions than most modern Greens are prepared to contemplate. To take only the most obvious examples, whereas many Greens wish to weaken the power relations inherent in industrial capitalism, few are prepared to contemplate abolishing the ultimate repository of power – the state. And whereas many Greens denounce the environmental consequences of market forces, few have the political stomach to demand an end to the monetary economy entirely. On both these scores, the 'pure anarchists' pursued the logic of their arguments to unflinchingly Green conclusions.

Let us restate this in another fashion. Dobson makes it a defining feature of Greens that their politics proceed from a description of the limits to growth. Having established to their own satisfaction that the planet cannot take many more years of ecological damage on the scale inflicted by industrial capitalism, Greens then proceed to devise the measures needed to ensure ecological sustainability. Such measures can range from authoritarian to libertarian. Dobson borrows Tim O'Riordan's classification of the various Green responses into the following four broad categories: (i) demanding a 'new global order'; (ii) relying on 'centralised authoritarianism'; (iii) advocating an 'authoritarian commune' as the unit of social organisation; and (iv) turning to an 'anarchist solution' in the shape of 'the self-reliant community modelled on anarchist lines'.[5]

We can see that anarchism is presented here as one possible conclusion that can be drawn from the fundamental Green premise of 'limits to growth'. Moreover, it is interesting to note that Dobson himself clearly favours this conclusion to the other Green alternatives on offer: 'the closest approximation of the four positions described above to the centre of gravity of a Green sustainable society is the last one: the so-called "anarchist solution".'[6] To be fair to those Greens who locate themselves at this 'centre of gravity', one ought to point out that many wish to avoid Green being collapsed into anarchism and that, like Dobson, they therefore term their preferred Green alternative 'anarchistic' rather than purely 'anarchist'. Nevertheless, it remains the case that such Greens' train of thought leads them from a Green premise towards anarchism, even if, in the typically Green manner to which I referred earlier, they stop short of wholeheartedly demanding the abolition of either money or the state. If, as we have seen, the flow of ideas can run from Green towards anarchism, is there any logical reason why the current cannot be reversed – *from* anarchism *towards* Green? This is a rhetorical question because, as I hope to demonstrate, the Japanese 'pure anarchists' provide us with empirical evidence that this can indeed be the case.

## JAPANESE 'PURE ANARCHISM'

The primary motivation of the 'pure anarchists' lay in their desire to achieve anarchist communism. They wished to abolish capitalism, destroy the state and create in their place a decentralised society of freely associated communes, each of which would be largely self-supporting. With this as their goal, the 'pure anarchists' then proceeded to ask themselves how this might be brought about within the context of Japanese society in the 1920s and 1930s. The farming villages were judged to provide the physical structure within which the new social form of the free communes could take shape. However, the villages were being increasingly impoverished, since the strategy of the ruling class for Japan's capitalist development after 1868 had been to industrialise by transferring wealth from the countryside to the rapidly expanding, and hence overpopulated, cities.

The 'pure anarchists' considered that the cities were exploiting the rural areas and they judged modern industry to be inherently authoritarian, hierarchical and alienating. Hence the 'pure anarchists' regarded as a non-starter the idea that the workers should take over 'their' industries and run them in their own interests. Industry had to be dismembered, the cities had to be dissolved, and the workers should move back to the villages. It was adherence to this strategy which earned the majority of Japanese anarchists in this period the epithet 'pure', so as to distinguish them from the minority of anarchist syndicalists, who advocated 'the mines to the miners', 'the mills to the millworkers' and so forth.

Opposition to industrialisation and urbanisation triggered the criticism, which was often directed at the 'pure anarchists', that they were opposed to scientific progress. Hatta Shūzō [ 八太舩三 ] (1886–1934), the principal theoretician of the 'pure anarchists', met this criticism by developing a systematic critique of science, which encompassed its goals, methods and, above all, the degree to which it served capitalism's interests. This distrust of science is a striking example of the way in which the 'pure anarchists' broke new ground by overstepping the boundaries of European anarchist thought. The principal external influences acting on the 'pure anarchists' were the theoretical writings of the great Russian anarchist communist Peter Kropotkin (1842–1921). Kropotkin remained throughout his life a worshipper at the altar of science and consequently sought to imbue anarchism with scientific methodology. As he wrote in *Modern Science and Anarchism*:

Anarchism is a world-concept based upon a mechanical explanation of all phenomena, embracing the whole of nature – that is, including in it the life of human societies and their economic, political and moral problems. Its method of investigation is that of the exact natural sciences, and, if it pretends to be scientific, every conclusion it comes to must be verified by the method by which every scientific conclusion must be verified. Its aim is to construct a synthetic philosophy comprehending in one generalisation all the phenomena of nature – and therefore also the life of societies.[7]

Unlike Kropotkin, Hatta rejected the temptation to locate anarchism as the terrain of Baconian science. As we shall see, he dismissed the claims of science to be objective and value-free, arguing instead that science was a system of knowledge which was specific to a particular historical epoch and a particular set of class interests.

Although Hatta refused to accept that scientism provided an adequate theoretical basis for the struggle for anarchist communism, he saw no reason to reject the method, which Kropotkin had employed in *Mutual Aid*, of basing decisions on how human society should be organised on observations of animals in their natural environment. As is well known, in *Mutual Aid* Kropotkin sought to counter the Social Darwinist contention that capitalist competition is nothing but the biological struggle for survival, with weapons such as price cutting and entrepreneurial flair being substituted for claws and fangs. Kropotkin marshalled evidence in order to demonstrate that in the natural environment those species prosper which are most adept at practising reciprocal support and mutual aid. The thesis that mutual aid serves the species better than a universal war of all against all was then extended from the world of nature into human society. This idea that nature holds lessons for humans was accepted by the 'pure anarchists' and used by their propagandists, such as Hatta, to warn the people of their day that, unless those lessons were heeded, catastrophe lay ahead. In an article on 'The Cooperative Life of Animals (on Social Solidarity)', which Hatta wrote in 1930, we find:

> However, is humankind not on the brink of future destruction? Terrifying war, which is not to be found among those very animals, and exploitation, which cannot possibly be found among them, are even now leading humankind towards the abyss of extinction. If humans do not learn from the animals, do not listen to the animals, they will, by carrying on in their present fashion, cease to exist on the earth.[8]

Perhaps it will be objected that the apparently Green sentiments expressed here are not really so because they do not proceed from the premise of 'the limits to growth'.

Certainly, what seem to have been uppermost in Hatta's mind when he wrote this article were the perceived threats of economic crisis and impending war, rather than the depletion of resources or the consequences of pollution (not that these corollaries of industrialisation were by any means unknown in pre-war Japan, of course). Even conceding this, however, one still might reasonably argue that what this demonstrates is not that the 'pure anarchists' failed the Green test because of the premises from which their arguments proceeded, but that, starting from different premises to many modern Greens, they nevertheless arrived at conclusions which were no less Green for that reason. At first glance, the argument might seem to have reached stalemate there, unable to progress beyond the point where one simply declares that 'it all depends on what one means by Green'. However, there is, I believe, a way of nudging it beyond this point. The acid test seems to me to lie in the question 'Would the ideas expressed in the passage above be acceptably Green if they had proceeded from "the limits to growth" premise?' If the answer Greens would give to this question is affirmative, the matter is clinched for me. Green lies in the changes one seeks to bring about and the methods one seeks to employ, not in the route which one's ideas have traversed in order to commit oneself to a Green course of action.

The 'pure anarchists' sought to alter the scale and purpose of production, even if their reasons for doing so lay in their determination to end what they saw as the city's exploitation of the village rather than the ecological consequences of overproduction. In the Village Youth Association's ( 農村青年社/Nōson Seinensha) manifesto *Appeal to the Peasants*, which was published in 1931, a strategy of rural revolution was put forward, whereby the villages could be transformed into free communes. The key to this transformation was for the villages to cease producing for sale and to switch their efforts to supplying their own needs directly. The peasants were urged to grow food not for sale on the urban market but for consumption within the village. Similarly, they were to supply their other needs through handicrafts and locally based workshops, rather than relying on manufactured articles from the cities. If such changes were implemented, it was asked, would not the villages cease to be mere appendages of the cities engaged in the production of cash crops and could they not become

79

genuine communities from which all social divisions had been eradicated: 'why can't money disappear from the village and the village live as one big family?'[9]

One strikingly Green facet of the overall transformation that was advocated in *Appeal to the Peasants* was the recommendation that the peasants should cease to use commercial fertilisers. This was not because Miyazaki Akira [宮崎晃] (1889–1977), the author of *Appeal to the Peasants*, feared the pollution which arises when nitrates pass into the water supply. On the contrary, there is no indication that he was aware that the use of commercial fertilisers had harmful ecological effects. What he was acutely aware of were the *social* effects of the peasants resorting to commercial fertilisers. Once they started to purchase fertilisers, they were enmeshed in a web of buying and selling relationships, needing to produce crops for sale in order to acquire the money with which to obtain the means to farm. Miyazaki insisted that good crops could be produced by using natural fertilisers (in the Japanese context, this meant primarily nightsoil), so the means to break out of the vicious circle of commercial agriculture lay in the peasants' lavatories. Establishing a natural cycle of growing crops, consuming them as food, collecting the resulting excrement and enriching the soil with this was seen as an integral part of the anarchist communist project of transcending the antagonistic relationships which existed between buyer and seller, landlord and tenant, capitalist and worker, and thereby achieving communal solidarity.[10]

In the case of fertilisers, it was argued that natural substitutes could replace commercial products without having a major impact on the standard of living (using this term here in a conventional sense). Miyazaki recognised, however, that natural substitutes might not always be available if the peasants refused to purchase goods from the cities. The result might then well be that the peasants would have to do without, adjust their lifestyles, or even accept a poorer standard of living when measured by conventional criteria. To take a concrete example, there would be no kerosene for the lamps which lit most peasant houses or, in villages that were connected to the electricity network, the lights would go out if the bills were not paid. Miyazaki urged his peasant readers not to be discouraged by the resulting inconvenience. Kerosene lamps and electric lights are not essential, he maintained. As alternatives, the peasants could make their own candles, use vegetable oil, produce methane gas locally from organic waste, and so forth. If none of these were feasible, they could even adjust their rhythm of life in line with the hours of daylight.[11] Hence a possible outcome of abstaining from commercial interaction with the cities was that levels of consumption would be reduced. Even though such a reduction in consumption levels would have been from a much lower baseline than that which induces modern Greens to encourage the inhabitants of so-called advanced countries to consume less, Miyazaki and his comrades were not deterred. The kernel of their argument was that, even if life in anarchist communism were poorer in quantitative terms, qualitatively it would be richer and happier. It hardly needs to be added that a similar spirit and scale of values inform any number of modern Green writings.

In the next sections of this paper, I shall examine in greater detail some of the characteristics which gave 'pure anarchism' its Green hue. The theoretical issues which I have selected for more detailed attention here are the critique of science, the critique of the cities and the critique of productionism.

## THE CRITIQUE OF SCIENCE

It was Hatta who launched a front attack on science in a series of articles that he wrote for *Labour Movement* (労働運動 /Rôdô Undô) in 1927.[12] In these articles he announced his intention 'to prove that natural science is the enemy of the people and to give a detailed explanation of the fact that a new system of knowledge must be created'.[13] Hatta pointed out that when people talk about such 'wonders of science' as the radio, or the motor car or the electric tram (all of which were still novelties in Japanese cities in the 1920s), they overlook the fact that much of the misery of modern life is equally attributable to science. The regimenting of the work-force in factories and the phenomenon of people working endlessly in poverty are just as much the result of science's role in society as are spectacular inventions and handy gadgets.

Hatta's critique of science was embedded in an historical account of the changing forms of human knowledge. Among so-called primitive peoples, knowledge had various characteristics. Within their range of knowledge, it was that which was most important for maintaining life (knowledge of crops, knowledge of fire, and so forth) that was most highly valued. In other words, whatever contributed most to communal well-being was endowed with a spiritual aura. The other vital aspect of supposedly 'primitive' knowledge was that it was held in common by the community as a whole.

Hatta maintained that the forms taken by human knowledge change as society evolves. The common feature of all systems of knowledge found within class societies is that care is taken by the ruling classes to monopolise vital areas of knowledge so that they can be used as instruments of control. The principle of common knowledge is thus lost, as is the belief that whatever contributes most to communal well-being has the highest spiritual value. It is not necessary to go into the details of Hatta's classification of varieties of class knowledge, but essentially Hatta's argument was that, although knowledge could assume various forms in different class societies, a constant feature which it exhibited was that it was jealously guarded by a minority so as to serve their interests. In the European Middle Ages, for example, knowledge took the form of religious dogma and was employed by the ruling class to mystify the people, discourage dissent and justify the élite's power and privileges.

Hatta held that science was not knowledge as such but merely one variety of class knowledge. It was not an historical accident that the rise of science coincided with the consolidation and expansion of capitalism. On the contrary, being a class society, capitalism needed a form of knowledge which was monopolised by specialists ('scientists'), was therefore inaccessible to the mass of the people, and could be used as an allegedly neutral and value-free arbiter whenever people's interests were sacrificed in the name of 'progress'. The route by which science achieved its victory over religious dogma lay through the rise of rationalism and the epoch of the Enlightenment, neither of which Hatta held in high regard. He did not dispute that there had been an advance in human understanding when, for example, it was grasped that the planet turns on its axis, rather than the sun rising in the East and setting in the West. On the other hand, the price which had been exacted for this advance in understanding was the emergence of 'the belief in an all-powerful reason' (理性万能主義 /risei bannōshugi/). Humans were now perceived as insignificant in the face of a natural universe which works according to its own laws: 'Giant nature (大自然 /dai shizen) becomes an enormous machine which operates without concern for human happiness or misery and, irrespective of whether they are laughing or crying, in the face of this machine of giant nature, human beings become creatures devoid of any authority.'[14]

The danger inherent in this attitude was that scientists come to erect 'natural laws' which, because they are considered to be expressions of incontrovertible reason, take on the role of sources of authority to which people have no option but to submit. Hatta was suspicious of external authority in any shape, no matter whether it took the form of rulers and their self-serving laws or science and its 'natural laws'. His contention was that 'natural laws' are not natural phenomena existing independently of humans. 'What are natural laws?', he asked, and replied: 'They are nothing more than things which reduce observed reality to an extremely simple form for the sake of economic convenience in human thought.' Even 'nature' is a product of human thought – a concept and an abstraction: 'Both what is called nature and natural laws were created by humans for the sake of humans. Humans were not created for the sake of nature and natural laws.'[15] Their being the products of human minds means that so-called 'natural laws' are fallible and should be treated with scepticism, rather than as forces to which people have no option but to conform.

The conclusion which Hatta drew from his study of science was that 'we must build a new social system, create a new system of knowledge, and get rid of science'.[16] He saw science as operating on the principle of universality (普遍性 / fuhensei). It is based on mathematics, in the sense that it relies on methods such as quantitative assessment and establishing numerically-derived norms, which are to be enforced with scant regard for local conditions and exceptional circumstances. In place of science, Hatta looked to the emergence of a new system of anarchist communist knowledge which would adopt specificity (特殊性 /tokushusei) as its fundamental principle. For that reason, he thought that the geographical rather than the mathematical metaphor came closest to capturing the essence of anarchist communist knowledge. The form of knowledge which he favoured was one which was, above all, sensitive to local circumstances and conditions: 'Like the people of ancient times, we should take as our starting point the knowledge which relates to the land on which we live in each district.'[17] The people of each locality were to live a life of self-support and self-sufficiency, and they would absorb that knowledge and engage in that study which enabled them to satisfy their needs with the minimum of labour. Universality was not to be rejected out of hand just because it was such a prominent feature of science. It could be assimilated into the new system of knowledge, but only to the extent that it contributed to specificity, locality, practical application and happiness. Universality would not be allowed to dictate blindly, as it was wont to do under the rule of science at the service of capitalism.

Hatta's critique of science is itself open to criticism on a number of counts. For instance, in his enthusiasm for a new system of knowledge, he overlooks the danger that its guiding principle of specificity might lead to a mean-spirited, narrow localism. There was a possibility, which Hatta did not sufficiently recognise, that the local community's intellectual universe might not extend beyond the immediate commune, its concerns and preoccupations. However, my purpose here is not to evaluate Hatta's critique of science in terms of its intellectual merit, but merely to draw attention to its affinity with Green theory. Criticism of science in the Bacon-Descartes-Newton mode is widespread among modern Greens and stood at the heart of Hatta's writings on the subject. Similarly, most modern Greens would share Hatta's unease with the intellectual assumptions which pervaded the ideology of the Enlightenment. The image of nature as a giant mechanism whose remorselessly operating processes are the manifestations of implacable reason is as repellent to most Greens as it was to Hatta. Nor does the point need to be laboured that comments such as 'we should take as our starting point the knowledge which relates to the land on which we live in each district' would fit comfortably into any number of modern Green texts. Even the criticism that localism might have a narrowing effect on people's intellectual horizons has been directed at modern Green thought. Despite these similarities, one would not wish to claim that, in every respect, the 'pure anarchist' critique of science is identical to the corresponding area of modern Green thought. Hatta's views on 'nature' spring to mind in this regard. Once again, however, the point can legitimately be made that the 'pure anarchist' critique of science led to startlingly Green conclusions despite (or rather, just because of) the anarchist communist philosophical foundation which underpinned it.

## THE CRITIQUE OF THE CITIES

As pre-war Japan moved ever farther down the path towards becoming an industrialised society, opposition to this development took various forms, only one of which was 'pure anarchism'. Another manifestation of opposition to industrialisation was the doctrine of *nōhonshugi* (農本主義) (literally 'agriculture-as-the-root-ism'). *Nōhonshugi* ideologues argued that the cities were exploiting the countryside and sought political change of a type that would ensure that agriculture was accorded precedence over industry. *Nōhonshugi* was one of the streams that fed into the swelling torrent of right-wing militarism which finally engulfed Japan in the 1930s. As with the advocates of *nōhonshugi*, the 'pure anarchists' took the view that the cities were exploiting the countryside. However, their preferred solution lay not in reversing that exploitative relationship so that the villages came out on top, but in dissolving the urban centres and hence transcending the division between town and country.

In the eyes of the 'pure anarchists', industrial capitalism worked in such a fashion that the entire urban population benefited from the exploitation of the peasantry. Since they held that rural produce exchanged on unequal terms with manufactured goods, it followed that even the urban proletarians, exploited though they were by the capitalists, still benefited from relatively cheap food at the peasants' expense. Conversely, the 'pure anarchists' maintained that, when workers secured wage rises, the costs were passed on to the peasants in the form of more expensive manufactured goods. From the standpoint of the 'pure anarchists', the essential point to grasp was that, whereas the peasants were invariably at the bottom of a pile which had the urban capitalists at its apex, exploitation was built into capitalism so that everyone (including the poorest peasant) was, potentially or actually, an exploiter of everybody else. The root cause of exploitation lay in inequality of power; and the cities were the ultimate *foci* of exploitation because both economic and political power gravitated towards these centres. From their earliest origins, cities had always been centres of authority, within which those who wielded power profited at the expense of the surrounding country-side. Hence the 'pure anarchists' argued that any revolution which intended to leave the cities intact would be unable to prevent the emergence of new relationships based on power and exploitation. As the *Appeal to the Peasants* put it:

> Even though the established power might be toppled, as long as the cities exist, those cities must seek provisions in the villages. Even if power is done away with, it is unavoidable that power will be born again in order to requisition provisions, and a point will be reached where government will be re-established.[18]

In his influential lecture series on social problems in the farming villages, which was published as a booklet in 1928, Hatta asserted that society was confronted by a major crisis because people were no longer living naturally and engaging in agriculture. Cities were displacing villages and, for Hatta, the severing of people's links with the land constituted a disease which was eating at the very heart of society. The 'pure anarchists' held that, as objects of exploitation, both peasants and urban workers had an interest in revolution. However, while 'the land to the peasants' represented a justifiable aspiration for the farming communities, 'the factories to the workers' was a false goal for the urban proletariat. The object of the workers' struggles should be to dissolve the cities, forcefully end large-scale production, where their every movement was programmed according to the division of labour, and disperse into the countryside. Taking their skills with them into the countryside, the workers could set up workshops in rural settings and hence achieve the balance between agriculture and small-scale industry which Kropotkin had described in *Fields, Factories and Workshops*. Although this proposed method of transforming society owed something to Kropotkin, it was both innovative and authentically Japanese in other respects. Whereas Kropotkin, for all his enthusiasm for the land, had expected the revolution to progress from the cities to the countryside, the 'pure anarchists' pinned their revolutionary hopes primarily on the peasants, both because of the intensity of their exploitation and because of certain characteristics of village life which were judged to reinforce their tendency towards cooperation and their sense of community. Foremost among these features of peasant life were the communal maintenance of the irrigation system and the custom of cooperative labour at transplanting time, without which rice cultivation was impossible:

> In the present era of capitalism, selfish egoism has penetrated even into the villages, but all the same the farming village cannot exist unless, as a village, it practises cooperative irrigation and cooperative endeavour. When the peasants organise a village by means of cooperative and communal endeavour, they possess a power which does not depend on the law or on orders, but which is the power of human beings to organise a natural society and to strive for a cooperative existence and common prosperity – a natural power which human beings have been endowed with from ancient times.[19]

What we see in the 'pure anarchist' critique of the cities is a programme of deurbanisation as thorough as any envisaged by modern Greens. But it is equally apparent that the 'pure anarchists' came to advocate this strategy of social transformation due to a sequence of ideas which started with their analysis of exploitation. In other words, their Green-ness lay in the point at which they arrived, rather than in the ideas which transported them there.

THE CRITIQUE OF PRODUCTIONISM

It is an article of faith among modern Greens that consumption and production must be cut back so as to rescue the environment and achieve a sustainable society. In the light of the miserable living conditions experienced by both peasants and workers in pre-war Japan, it is hardly surprising that the 'pure anarchists' did not approach the question of how to reorganise production with the primary intention of reducing consumption. However, they were keenly aware that capitalism is a social system which exhibits a compulsive need to expand production and, in their view, the principal means by which capitalism pursues this goal lies in the division of labour. For the 'pure anarchists', the division of labour was much more than an economic device for raising the efficiency (in capitalist terms) of production. It was also the ultimate source of authority.

The 'pure anarchists' argued that the division of labour destroys social solidarity, goes hand in hand with class divisions, and makes the existence of the state inevitable. This was, in fact, the basis of the 'pure anarchists' criticism of those anarchists who favoured a syndicalist strategy. The anarchist syndicalists sought to organise the workforce factory by factory and industry by industry, but this had the effect of reproducing within the unions capitalism's own division of labour. Moreover, since the anarchist syndicalists proposed that the unions should administer the society of the future, they were pursuing a strategy which would have preserved the division of labour even after the revolution. The 'pure anarchists' contended that, were this to occur, even in post-revolutionary society workers would seek to benefit 'their' factory or 'their' industry at the expense of others. The resulting social tensions could then only be held in check by some form of supervising body which stood above the sectional interests spawned by the division of labour. This, however, would spell disaster for the basic anarchist project, because what else would this supervisory body be than the re-emergent state? Hatta described this sequence of events in a series of articles entitled 'Let's Establish Our Own Economics' (1929–30).

> Where the division of labour occurs, exchange takes place. Where exchange takes place, a medium of exchange – in other words, money (or labour vouchers) – comes into existence. And money stands in need of a basis of centralised power (government). The development of money naturally leads to the development of government.[20]

As we have already seen, the society which the 'pure anarchists' struggled to achieve was a decentralised federation of free communes. By engaging in both agriculture and a wide range of handicrafts and small-scale industries, it was anticipated that the communes would achieve a high degree of self-sufficiency and, at the same time, transcend the social division of labour. It was not only the way in which production was organised that was intended to change, but also the purpose of production. Whereas the 'pure anarchists' characterised capitalism as a society which 'takes production as its basis', anarchist communism was to 'take consumption as its basis'. This latter formula might well set alarm bells ringing with modern Greens, since it could (mistakenly) be interpreted as a society whose *raison d'être* lies in consumption. However, what the 'pure anarchists' intended to convey by this expression was that, in contrast to the priority which capitalism necessarily accords to expanding the means of production, decisions about what to produce, how to produce and how much to produce would in anarchist communism all be functions of prior deliberations on consumption. In fact, there is a remarkable similarity of approach in the 'pure anarchist' belief that the economic cycle should start with consumption and Dobson's contention that: 'Of these four [resource depletion, production, consumption and waste] . . . it seems to me that consumption provides the most useful starting-point for discussion. In the first place this is because the other three terms are founded upon the existence and persistence of consumption: consumption implies depletion implies production implies waste.'[21]

Nevertheless, the 'pure anarchists' were not ascetics and certainly believed that anarchist communism would enable people to live a more comfortable life than workers and peasants endured in Japan in the 1920s and 1930s. Yet even though the 'pure anarchists' expected that the mass of the people would be better clothed, housed and fed in anarchist communism than under the capitalism which then existed, we should not overlook the fact that a social and economic structure consisting of decentralised, part agricultural/part small-scale industrial communes would have set definite limits on attainable levels of production. To mention but one example: no commune would have had the where-withal for the mass production of motor cars, nor would its members have had any need for them. Thus the intensive industrial development which Japan subsequently experienced, and the massive environmental destruction which has accompanied it, would have been prevented if the 'pure anarchists' had won in their life-and-death struggle with the forces of capital and the state.

Be that as it may, it again needs to be emphasised that what primarily motivated the 'pure anarchists' was not the material advantages that anarchist communism might or might not bring, but the *qualitative* improvement in people's lives that they expected. The 'pure anarchists' readily conceded that capitalism was well suited to promoting economic growth, but they maintained that true economic well-being does not lie in churning out ever greater quantities of commodities. Hatta succinctly expressed this fundamental criticism of capitalism in the following passage from 'Let's Establish Our Own Economics':

> Since the mode of production which has prevailed up till now is one which determines the starting point of the economic process, the prime question becomes how to raise the level of production, and not how to produce and what to produce. As a result, there is no alternative to proceeding on the basis of the division of labour. This is because nothing raises the level of production so much as the division of labour. However, humankind cannot advance to happiness by means of a large volume of production.[22]

Which modern Green could not echo this sentiment?

## CONCLUSION

One can see why there is a tendency among modern Greens to draw a line separating their movement from radical movements in the past. It is obviously tempting for Greens to attempt to divorce themselves from past failures and to project an image of themselves as an entirely new movement which is untainted by any association with previous defeats. However, I think this is a temptation which Greens would be well advised to reject for at least two reasons. First, because it is simply untrue that their ideas and aspirations are unrelated to those of past movements. In this paper I have tried to establish the Green credentials of a movement which although at its height measured its support in tens of thousands, was destroyed by the Japanese state more than 50 years ago. In focusing attention on the Japanese 'pure anarchists' of the 1920s and 1930s, I do not wish to suggest that they were unique in advocating, ahead of their time, many of the changes for which Greens are now campaigning. I have merely used the 'pure anarchists' as a specific example of one movement among probably many which were Green before the term was even coined. Others could no doubt make the same points as I have done by reference to other movements in other parts of the world which would lend themselves to the exercise.

The second reason why, in my view, modern Greens need to pay greater attention to those movements in the past with which they have an affinity is that there are lessons which can be learnt from doing so. In my account, I suggested that, in some respects, the 'pure anarchists' were more consistently Green than are most modern Greens. It is surprising and depressing that, for all their self-proclaimed iconoclasm, so many modern Greens cling to illusions about the monetary economy and the state. Far from getting to the root of the ecological problem, typically Green proposals to 'make the polluters pay' are based on the assumption that the monetary economy should persist. Yet if the pursuit of monetary profit is not the prime cause of pollution, what is? Similarly, calls for an 'ecologically sound system of government' are apparently oblivious of the environmental record of governments everywhere. Power relations are always a factor in ecological damage, and it is illogical to imagine that the damage can be redressed by resorting to yet more power in the shape of government. Greens would find the writings of the Japanese 'pure anarchists' instructive in both these regards.

Finally, there is a lesson to be learnt from the eventual fate of the 'pure anarchist' movement. Throughout the existence of their movement, the 'pure anarchists' experienced harassment at every turn. Their public meetings were broken up, their publications suppressed and their members imprisoned. Eventually in 1935 there was a mass round-up of the anarchists and their organisations were banned entirely. Modern Greens could well reflect on the similar likelihood that, if their movement reaches the point where it is threatening the power and privileges of those at the apex of the polluting society, they can expect no quarter.

## NOTES

1. I am grateful to Neil Carter and Andrew Dobson for kindly commenting on an earlier version of this paper.
2. Andrew Dobson, *Green Political Thought* (London: Unwin Hyman, 1990) p. 32.
3. *Ibid.*, p. 33.
4. *Ibid.*, pp. 33–4.
5. Tim O'Riordan, *Environmentalism* (London: Pion, 1976) pp. 303–7.
6. Dobson (1990) p. 83.
7. Roger N. Baldwin, *Kropotkin's Revolutionary Pamphlets* (New York: Dover, 1970) p. 150.
8. *Collected Works of Hatta Shuzo* 八太船三全集/*Hatta Shizō Zenshū*] (Tokyo: Kokushoku Sensensha, 1981) p. 136.
9. *Black Flag* ( /Kurohata) February 1931, p. 7.
10. *Ibid.* p. 8.

11. *Ibid.*
12. *Collected Works of Hatta Shuzo*, pp. 8–22.
13. *Ibid.* p. 8.
14. *Ibid.* p. 15.
15. *Ibid.* p. 20.
16. *Ibid.*
17. *Ibid.* pp. 20–1.
18. *Black Flag*, February 1931, p. 14.
19. *Collected Works of Hatta Shuzo*, p. 284.
20. *Ibid.* p. 116.
21. Dobson (1980) p. 89.
22. *Collected Works of Hatta Shuzo*, p. 129.

# 7

# The status of the Emperor as a national symbol in the fifteen-year war period 1931–1945*

OLAVI K. FÄLT

MY AIM HERE is to analyse the use made of the crucial and highly exceptional position of the Emperor in the Japanese cultural tradition as a national symbol for the purposes of public debate during the period 1931–45, i.e. from the outbreak of the Manchurian Incident to the Japanese surrender, and to determine in what way it reflected the various aspirations, hopes and expectations that prevailed at the time. The material for this, which is part of a more extensive piece of research in terms both of time-scale and sources, has been obtained from two English-language newspapers owned by the Japanese, the *Japan Times & Mail* (JT & M), known from 1943 onwards as the *Nippon Times* (NT) and the *Osaka Mainichi & Tokyo Nichi Nichi* (OM & TNN), or simply the *Mainichi* after 1943. The points in time to be examined are those when the Emperor, either his person, the office or the dynasty, was particularly prominent in the news, principally the Emperor's birthday, *Tenchō-setsu*, 29 April, and Japan's mythological Foundation Day, *Kigen-setsu* (*kenkokusai*), 11 February, dating from 660 BC.

I have observed in earlier research concerned with the Taishō period (1912–1926) that these newspapers tended to emphasise a spirit of democracy and international cooperation in their references to the Emperor and his office.[1] Changes were detectable by the end of the 1920s and the early 1930s, however, above all in the assignment of a new prominence to national values. The reason I have prelimi-

---

* Translated by Malcolm Hicks

narily stated for this was the increase in external pressure at that time under the influence of both the rise of nationalist feeling in China and the reluctant and even hostile attitude of the Western powers towards Japanese immigrants, together with internal, especially economic, problems.[2]

## THE MANCHURIAN INCIDENT AND THE RISE OF NATIONALISM

The internal changes that occurred as a consequence of the Manchurian Incident are reflected well in the leading article published by the JT & M on the eve of *Kigen-setsu* in 1932, in which it analysed the background to the strong position of the military in Japan in fairly universal terms by explaining how the current situation facilitated the rise of such a group to power. It pointed out that the war psychosis fostered by the army and navy was likely to fall on receptive ears, as the people no longer believed in the abilities of the 'political game' to solve the country's problems. Whatever the pacifists might say about the misguided ideas of the military representatives, they could not question their sincerity, patriotism and honesty.[3]

Although the paper adopted an understanding attitude towards the new political situation, it was more inclined to criticise the political parties than to praise the armed forces, and in this sense it evidently was not prepared to confess to being a victim of the war psychosis but rather tried to be a discreet critic of it. This was also apparent from the paper's comments at the time of the Emperor's birthday that year, when it sought support for its own views on the status of the Emperor, claiming that since the nation had scarcely ever gone through such a critical period as the present one, it was natural that it should turn to the Emperor for inspiration and advice, especially when the ruling house concerned was without peer in world history as far as its continuity and longevity were concerned.[4]

Having in this way created a firm foundation for its criticism, as it were, the paper went on to point out that it was important to remember at that time, when so much emphasis was being laid on nationalism, that the fundamental institutions of the Empire had never been coloured by an antipathy for foreigners. It quoted the exhortation of the late Emperor Meiji that the Japanese should seek for knowledge in every corner of the world, and pointed out how the present Emperor, many members of the Imperial Family and those subjects of theirs who had studied and travelled abroad had done precisely that.[5]

The JT & M touched upon the rise in patriotism brought about by the international crisis once again when referring to the celebration of *Kigen-setsu* in 1933,[6] at precisely the time when the highly critical Lytton Report on Japan's Manchurian policy was being debated in the League of Nations. The paper in fact played its part in fostering this patriotism by going over the events connected with the mythical emergence of Japan and its first Emperor, Jimmu, and indicating quite overtly that the commemoration of *Kigen-setsu* was of particular significance to the nation in the current context.[7]

The OM & TNN meanwhile emphasised the role of the Emperor as a guide to the nation through the ages and the people's unswerving loyalty to him,[8] adopting in principle much the same tone as in earlier years. Of particular interest in this respect was the appreciation and gratitude expressed by the paper on the occasion of the Emperor's birthday in 1933 that he was able to act as a guiding force for the nation in the face of all its difficulties, especially following its resignation from the League of Nations. The paper then went on to refer to the Imperial rescript urging both the civil authorities and the military to attend to their own particular duties.[9] This was evidently intended as a criticism of the aspirations to political hegemony entertained in military circles. As Ian Nish has indicated, the rescript was in fact so critical of the military that the first version had to be rejected in the face of vehement army protest. The original wording had been that the civil and military authorities should work in harmony, each in its own sector, and avoid interference in each other's affairs.[10]

The OM & TNN nevertheless continued its policy of placing major emphasis on national values, as emerged in connection with the *Kigen-setsu* celebrations in 1934, which gained especial significance on account of the birth of the Crown Prince the previous December.[11] The paper in any case evidently wished to add more than usual weight to the occasion by drawing its reader's attention to certain matters of contemporary importance, including a call for the Shōwa period to be recognised on a par with the Meiji Restoration and the times of the Emperor Jimmu in the sense of national unity, a quality which the paper observed to be lamentably lacking at the time. It demanded that the whole nation should be united, but in a somewhat contradictory manner, also advised that care should be taken not to harm relations between Japan and those countries that were favourably disposed towards her. In other words, the nation should not listen to those who were trying to destroy its internal harmony nor those who were trying to undermine its relations with others.[12] The very inconsistency of the sentiments expressed by OM & TNN was in itself an indication of the difficulties being experienced in maintaining a balance between international cooperation and the demands of the military.

The birth of the Crown Prince came up again on the occasion of the Emperor's birthday in 1934, when the paper mentioned the Emperor's efforts to promote welfare in all aspects of his country's life, but 'with special interest in military affairs',[13] a comment which presumably reflected the increased influence of the military and the country's territorial expansion onto the mainland.

Writing in connection with the birthday celebrations in 1935, the JT & M attempted to counteract the considerable upsurge of nationalist feeling prevalent at that time by pointing out how the occasion should be one of joy and gratitude towards the Emperor and not a manifestation of nationalism and extremist sentiments.[14] The same notion also emerged on the corresponding occasion a year later, coming just two months after the dramatic attempt at a *coup d'état* in which many leading politicians and soldiers of a more moderate disposition who had been opposed to a more active foreign policy and an increase in the military budgets had been killed.[15] The paper extolled the Emperor by speaking of the influence of the Imperial throne in guiding the nation on a balanced course and guaranteeing peace and happiness throughout its history. People had looked on their Emperor at times of both peace and unrest not only as their ruler but also as the power responsible for their fate, and this had been seen once again in the events of 26 February.[16]

The OM & TNN similarly warned of the dangers of nationalism in its *Kigen-setsu* commentary of 1936 by drawing attention to the fact that an ardent nationalist fervour would not lead anywhere, that it was not guided by reason and that it could not be manifested in a well-balanced manner.[17] The paper then returned to the same theme in the spring, on account of the attempted *coup*, maintaining that this latter event had plunged the nation into a deeper crisis than ever and that the eventual outcome seemed highly unpredictable. Its earlier nationalistic views were now much more restrained as a result of the pressure of recent events. It admittedly showed appreciation of the speed with which the ruler had resolved the attempted *coup*, but viewed the prospects for managing the country's future affairs with considerable anxiety. A successful outcome called for calm and common sense, it claimed, quoting the words of its own *Kigen-setsu* article on the need for careful, balanced reflection and democratic participation: 'Simultaneously, we earnestly desire that the people carefully reflect as to the means through which to clarify the form of our state.'[18] A further indication of the paper's anxiety may well have been the repeated reference to the growing role of military matters in the Emperor's duties: 'We are filled with trepidation on learning that His Majesty is incessantly attending to military affairs'.[19]

Our resulting interpretation is thus that while the JT & M reacted to the increased tension by adopting a somewhat more nationalistic tone, the OM & TNN backed down from its previous stance to some extent, began to stress deliberation and the importance of democratic procedures in deciding on the nation's affairs, and in general attempted to moderate the heightened atmosphere of nationalistic fervour. The role of the Emperor in this connection remained that of a symbol of loyalty and unity, although the nationalist extremism and blatant militarism which was beginning to be associated with this loyalty aroused fears in the minds of its commentators.

The overthrow of the attempted *coup* did not mean that Japan's internal and external crisis had come to an end, however. On the contrary, tension only mounted further. This was reflected in the remark by the JT & M in spring 1937, on the occasion of the ceremony at the shrine of Yasukuni, held annually at the end of April for the purpose of elevating those who had died in the defence of their country in the course of the year as gods to be preserved in the shrine. The paper emphasised how the Emperor occupied a position at the centre of national life and everyone worked for the success of the Imperial Family. Even one's own life was not so valuable that it could not be laid down in the service of the Emperor and the nation, and in fact millions of people were ready to do just this at any time, for although their death would bring sorrow to those around them, they were consoled greatly by the thought that the departed were preserved as gods and pillars of the nation in the shrine of Yasukuni and were attended there by the Emperor himself.[20]

When emphasising the close, almost supernatural bond between the Emperor and his people, the paper was evidently returning to the long tradition of Japanese nationalism, for the view it expressed was borrowed almost word for word from Yoshida Shōin (1830–1859), the greatest Imperial nationalist of the Tokugawa period, who had maintained that all the time the ruler existed, the nation existed, and if there was no ruler, there was no nation. He believed that the Emperor's will was supreme and that he was to be served until death. In other words, the whole nation was to be sacrificed if necessary in order to save its most essential features.[21]

Another clear sign of polarisation in internal affairs was the anxiety expressed by the OM & TNN at *Kigen-setsu* in the same year on account of the disarray in which the country found itself,[22] for it was at the moment that the conflict between the military circles and the representatives of the political parties was reaching a head in the form of an open rift in Parliament.[23] It then returned to the same theme of public confusion on the occasion of the Emperor's birthday in the spring, noting that the problem was the difficulty that each citizen experienced in expressing loyalty to the Imperial line in his own work. This was an obvious sign of the state of disarray that prevailed in Japan at that time. No one knew what constituted true loyalty to the Emperor, i.e. how the problems should be resolved, or which faction in the country best represented that loyalty.[24]

The paper's article devoted to the Emperor's birthday dealt with the Emperor's various functions, political, military, academic and cultural, more equally than the previous year, although again there was some emphasis on the crucial role of political and military matters: 'We are filled with trepidation on learning that His Majesty is incessantly attending to the political and military affairs . . .'[25]

The repeating of this comment may again be interpreted as discreet criticism of the hegemony aspirations harboured in military circles, i.e. of the assumption that it was the military that best represented loyalty to the Emperor. In other words, the OM & TNN would seem to be dressing up the existing trial of strength in internal affairs in the guise of the symbol of the Emperorship, in which form it consisted of a struggle as to what constituted true loyalty and who represented it, i.e. who exercised the real power in the country. In addition, the repeated references to the prime position of military matters in the duties of the Emperor may have even been an indirect criticism of the Emperor himself, although this would have indeed been a surprising state of affairs as all criticism of the Emperor was by tradition strictly forbidden, and all the more so under the condition of constantly tightening censorship in the 1930s. This censorship was not only designed to protect the Emperor, of course, but also the military circles.[26]

## THE OUTBREAK OF THE SINO-JAPANESE WAR AND INCREASING PRESSURE FOR UNITY

The outbreak of the Sino-Japanese War in summer 1937 meant an increase in the pressure exerted by nationalist circles on the political parties. The JT & M had its opportunity to defend the political system on 11 February 1938 when the *Kigen-setsu* celebrations also incorporated the 50th anniversary of the Japanese constitution. In the newspaper's opinion the unprecedented development that had taken place over the past 50 years was entirely attributable to the adoption of constitutional government. It attached great value to Parliament and the political parties as guarantors of the nation's well-being and regarded it as a disaster that they had not proved capable of fulfilling their constitutional obligations. By calling for improvements in this way, it was able to show sympathy with the critics while at the same time maintaining that to condemn constitutional government merely on the grounds that it did not work perfectly was to render an injustice to the constitution as such and to the will of the Emperor Meiji who first introduced it.[27] In other words, by referring to the Emperor Meiji and his legacy to the Japanese people the JT & M was able to exploit the status of the Emperor to defend the constitution against extremist attacks.

The OM & TNN did not set out so directly to defend the notion of constitutional government, but it did embrace the same sentiments in principle by demanding that attempts should be made to implement it in future and that, in accordance with the instructions laid down by the Emperor Meiji, the ministers of the government were personally responsible for this.[28]

As in the previous year, the JT & M commemorated the feast of the shrine of Yasukuni in a highly patriotic vein by remembering those who had laid down their lives for their country and honouring them as gods served by the Emperor and people alike.[29] With a war in progress, the traditional Emperor-centred outlook on the world was brought to the fore more prominently than ever and in a more belligerent manner. This was reflected in the greater weight laid on the Emperor's birthday and *Kigen-setsu* by both newspapers than in previous years and the emphasis laid on national unity in connection with them.[30]

As the war drew on, attempts were made to engage the people more closely in the war effort by appealing to the person of the Emperor. The OM & TNN mentioned in spring 1938 how, led by him, the troops had achieved major victories, but nevertheless exhorted the people to double their efforts in order to discharge successfully the enormous task that lay before the country.[31] At *Kigen-setsu* the following year it returned to this theme, likening the current reconstruction in East Asia to the founding of Japan by the Emperor Jimmu and looking forward to the successful completion of this work by the time of the commemoration of 2600 years of Japanese history the following year as the best possible way of marking the occasion.[32]

The emphasis placed on loyalty and unity reached its peak in the newspapers with the celebration of this anniversary on 11 February 1940. 'Japanese history means nothing if not the unity of the race', the JT & M wrote.[33] The OM & TNN, on the other hand, spoke of the reconstruction of East Asia as a task which could act in an exemplary manner as a manifestation of the respect for one's forefathers which formed such an important part of Japanese morality.[34] By the following year it was calling for perseverance of spirit and strong determination on the part of the people, but a new feature to enter the picture by this stage was a threat aimed at the United States that Japan's patience would soon be exhausted if that country did not abandon its arrogant attitude, the dagger held at Japan's throat, as the paper put it.[35]

## THE PACIFIC WAR – ABSOLUTE UNITY

Once Japan had begun its war against the United States and its allies, the Emperorship became a highly suitable symbol for the country's military objectives. Thus the first *Kigen-setsu* commemoration following the outbreak of war, that of February 1942, was marked by a eulogy in JT & M devoted to Japan's splendid victories. The day was referred to as the most significant *Kigen-setsu* in the country's history and the Japanese troops were likened to the great conquerors of world history: 'Our men are now among the world's immortals'.[36] The Empire was on the point of fulfilling the supreme mission in its history, that of liberating millions of its Asian brothers from Anglo-American persecution and founding a new world order in which the peoples of all the continents would be able to achieve their rightful national ideals.[37]

The OM & TNN was agreed that never before in its history had the Empire celebrated *Kigen-setsu* in the same atmosphere of confidence, hope, courage and satisfaction. The newspaper praised the victories gained in the past two months, estimating that such achievements would normally take at least a century, although it was not so confident of eventual victory as the JT & M, for in spite of the gains that had been made, the work of driving the United States and Britain out of East Asia had not yet been completed. This led the paper to recall the difficulties encountered by the Emperor Jimmu when creating a united Japan and to exhort every person to do all that he could to ensure that this great goal was achieved. It was a question of the fate of the entire Empire.[38]

Also linked with the news of Japanese expansion was the traditional notion of the global role of the Emperor, e.g. when the JT & M observed on his birthday in 1942 that the benefits of Imperial rule now extended to the eight corners of the world[39] and that it was the purpose of this rule to help every nation to find and secure its own place in the world. One promising sign of this was that the Philippines had 'spontaneously' adopted the Emperor's birthday as its own national day. Future prospects were also promising, for the nation had never before celebrated the Emperor's birthday with such nobility of heart and such expectations for the future as that spring. The people were more than contented with having to make sacrifices, in the knowledge that these were a very modest price to pay for the renewed happiness of East Asia. Seldom in history had the sword of justice been raised in a more noble cause than at that time.[40]

The OM & TNN took pains to emphasise the position of the Emperor as the focal point of all the efforts being made in the victorious war, and painted its readers a picture of his superhuman achievement: '. . . His Majesty the Emperor thus proceeds towards the consummation of the *greatest task since the beginning of the world*'.[41] [my italics]

By the following year, when the course of the war was beginning to shift in favour of the United States, the national days of commemoration provide a convenient opportunity to stimulate new faith and confidence in Japanese objectives and also indirectly warn her enemies of her striking power. In honour of *Kigen-setsu*, the JT & M, now the *Nippon Times* (NT), likened the current war to the expedition of the Emperor Jimmu over 2600 years earlier. Again it emphasised the global nature of the Emperorship by quoting Jimmu's mythical words that his aim was to see the whole world living in peace and harmony as if part of the same family, and pointed out, presumably to both friends and enemies alike, that Japan had never suffered defeat in her whole history, so that there was no reason now to suppose that the present gigantic undertaking would end in any less complete a victory than earlier.[42]

The OM & TNN, now known as the *Mainichi*, did not appeal to the example of the Emperor Jimmu to the same extent, but it still stressed that *Kigen-setsu* and the foundation of the Japanese nation by him were exceptionally prominent in people's minds that year, again evidently in an attempt to raise the nation's spirits in the midst of the increasingly arduous war.[43]

The NT returned to the theme of how Japan had never lost a war when writing on the occasion of *Kigen-setsu* in 1944, with fortunes declining all the time. It recalled the snatching of surprise victories over the Mongols, China and Russia, and emphasised the ability of the Japanese to make up for material disadvantages with their psychological strength, which was further increased by an awareness of the incontrovertible justice of their cause. Thus the paper hoped that the modern Japanese would prove the equals of their bold, patriotic forefathers in guiding their country through its crisis.[44] The seriousness of the situation was also reflected in the harsh language used by the *Mainichi* when referring to the United States and Britain as international 'pirates and bandits'.[45]

On the occasion of the Emperor's birthday that year, the NT alluded to the difficulty of defeating the Japanese by stating that the Emperor's birthday was a matter of significance for the country's enemies, reminding them of the unique blend of psychological and material strength which the Japanese possessed. One indication of this was the reverence they showed for their Emperor, on behalf of whom they were prepared to endure any hardships. His birthday also served to remind us that Japan was the only truly united people, united in a country that was without equal anywhere in the world.[46]

As the course of the war began to turn more obviously against Japan, this was reflected in the opinion of the *Mainichi*, which regarded it as a war devoted to the overthrow of a villainous enemy that was threatening the nation's very existence. The paper regarded the situation as more serious than at any previous time, and called on the people to do everything in their power, especially since the Emperor himself was setting a magnificent example, working from early in the morning to late at night for the good of the nation.[47]

By the time of *Kigen-setsu* in 1945 the *Mainichi* was forced to admit that fortunes had turned against Japan, but it still only regarded this as a passing phase, for the divine Nippon, whose fate had been contemporaneous with that of the heavens and the earth, would eventually emerge victorious. The celebration of *Kigen-setsu* and the giving of thanks to the Emperor Jimmu bound the people to the perpetuation of the welfare of the Imperial Family and the flourishing of the nation. The paper emphasised the necessity of winning the war, if only because its aims were those that had germinated in the days of the Emperor Jimmu, whose ideal had been to bestow eternal peace on the world and blessings upon the whole of mankind. The present war was merely an extension of these sentiments.[48] In other words, the war was a question of the most sacred values enshrined in Japanese tradition, the founding of the Japanese nation, its divinity and eternity. Thus the paper was committing everything that Japan possessed to the fight at this moment of national emergency.

Where the JT & M had claimed at the beginning of the war, in 1942, that that year's *Kigen-setsu* was the most significant ever, it was ready to write on the Emperor's birthday in 1945 that the country was now at the most decisive turning point in its history. The paper compared the relationship between the Emperor and his people in this situation with that between a father and his children, and, obviously quoting Yoshida Shōin again,[49] it referred to the mutual dependence between the people and the Emperor in the following words: 'There can be no Japanese nation without the Emperor any more than there can be family without a father; thus for the Japanese the Emperor and the State are connate and one.'[50] Although this was evidently another indication to the outside world of the difficulty of conquering Japan, it also concealed within it a fear for the continuity of the institution about which it was talking, for the paper went to demand quite openly that the Imperial throne should be retained even in the case of defeat, by reminding the enemy of the readiness of the Japanese to sacrifice their own lives on behalf of their Emperor:

> 'The enemy, recognising in the position of the Imperial Family the unique source of Japan's strength, would, if he could, *forcibly alter the basic loyalty of the Japanese nation* . . . The reign of the Imperial House is thus eternal and immortal *so long as a single subject of the Emperor should remain alive*.'[51] [my italics]

Loyalty, the paper claimed, conferred invincible strength on the Emperor and a divine blessing on Japan, a country which had no beginning or end, being eternal and immortal like the heavens and the earth,[52] as the Emperor Jimmu was said to have expressed it in his day.

The *Mainichi*, on the other hand, was much more reticent by that stage. It, too, regarded the crisis as the most serious in the nation's history, i.e. its mood, like that of the NT was the very opposite of what it had been three years earlier. It called for greater efforts, as before, but in a somewhat routine manner and with much the same phraseology, pointing out that the people should be a shield for the Imperial Family and that there had never been an Emperor who had worked so exclusively for the good of his people as the present one. Being obviously anxious for the fate of the Imperial Family in the event of defeat, the paper prayed for the continuity of the Imperial line.[53]

## CONCLUSIONS

It is evident from the above that the outbreak of the war with China in summer 1937 had a decisive influence on what matters the Emperorship was taken to symbolize. After that it was only in 1938, the anniversary of the constitution, that both newspapers set out to defend constitutional government in a liberal, democratic vein as they had done earlier, both before and after the Manchurian Incident. From then on allusions to the Emperor were made exclusively with the aim of strengthening the fighting spirit of the nation, in accordance with the official propaganda. As the prospect of defeat became more certain, still more energy was devoted to propagation of the traditional view, with increased references to the legendary founder of the Japanese nation, the Emperor Jimmu. Finally, towards the end of the war, anxiety began to be expressed for the fate of the Imperial throne as an institution in the event of defeat, appeals even being made to the enemy on its behalf.

## NOTES

1. Olavi K. Fält, 'Emperorship as a National Symbol in the Japan of the Taishō Era (1912–26)', *Western Interactions with Japan. Expansion, the Armed Forces & Readjustment 1859–1956*. Edited by Peter Lowe & Herman Moeshart. (Japan Library Ltd, Sandgate, Folkestone, Kent, Great Britain 1990), pp. 57–67.
2. Olavi K. Fält, *Keisarius kansallisena symboline Shōwa-kauden alun Japanisse 1926–1931* (Faravid 13.1989), pp. 89–99.
3. *Naval Ministry's Instructions*, JT & M 10.2.1931.
4. *Tencho-setsu*, JT & M 30.4.1932.
5. *Ibid.*
6. 'Entire Nation Joins in Observing Rites of *Kigen-setsu* Fete', JT & M 12.2.1933.
7. 'National Foundation Day', JT & M 12.2.1933.
8. 'The Imperial Birthday', OM & TNN 29.4.1932. 'Nippon's 2593rd Birth Anniversary Today; Nation to Observe *Kigen-setsu*', OM & TNN 11.2.1933.
9. 'The Emperor's Birthday', OM & TNN 29.4.1933.
10. Ian Nish, 'The Shōwa Emperor and the end of the Manchurian crisis' (*Japan Forum*, Vol. 1, No. 2, October 1989), p. 269.
11. OM & TNN 11.1.1934. See also *Kigen-setsu*. May Imperial Line Continue Forever', OM & TNN 11.2.1934.
12. *Kigen-setsu*, OM & TNN 11.2.1934.
13. 'Auspicious Occasion', OM & TNN 29.4.1934.
14. *Tencho-setsu*, JT & M 30.4.1935.
15. Ben-Ami Shillony, *Revolt in Japan. The Young Officers and the*

*February 26, 1936 Incident* (Princeton, New Jersey 1973), pp. 175–7.
16. *Tencho-setsu*, JT & M 30.4.1936.
17. *Kigen-setsu*, OM & TNN 11.2.1936.
18. *Ibid.*
19. *Tencho-setsu*, OM & TNN 29.4.1936.
20. 'Sacrifices Honoured', JT & M 28.4.1990.
21. Delmer M. Brown, *Nationalism in Japan. An Introductory Historical Analysis* (Berkeley and Los Angeles 1955), pp. 92–3.
22. *Kigen-setsu*, OM & TNN 11.2.1937.
23. See Olavi K. Fält, *'Fascism, Militarism or Japanism? The interpretation of the crisis years of 1930–1941 in the Japanese English-language press'* Studia Historica Septentrionalia 8. Societas Historica Finlandiae Septentrionalis, Rovaniemi, Jyväskylä 1985), pp. 88–101.
24. 'His Majesty's Birthday', OM & TNN 29.4.1937.
25. *Ibid.*
26. Richard H. Mitchell, *Censorship in Imperial Japan* (Princeton University Press, Princeton, New Jersey 1983), pp. 264–5.
27. 'Fifty Years of the Imperialist Constitution', JT & M 11.2.1938. See also Fält, *Fascism*, pp. 106–7.
28. *Kigen-setsu*, OM & TNN 11.2.1938.
29. 'Honour for the Dead', JT & M 27.4.1938.
30. 'Honouring the War Dead', JT & M 26.4.1939; 'Japan's Empire Day', JT & M 11.2.1941; 'Imperial Birthday', JT & M 29.4.1939; 'The Emperor's Birthday', JT & M 30.4.1940.
31. 'Long Live the Emperor', OM & TNN 29.4.1938.
32. *'Kigen-setsu* and New Asia', OM & TNN 11.2.1939.
33. '2600 Years of Japanese History', JT & M 11.2.1940.
34. Shingoro Takaishi, Celebration of *Kigen-setsu*, OM & TNN 11.2.1940. See also 'The Imperial Edict', OM & TNN 13.2.1940; '2601st Year of National Founding', OM & TNN 1.1.1941.
35. *Kigen-setsu* of 1941, OM & TNN 11.1.1941.
36. 'A Unique *Kigen-setsu*', JT & M 13.2.1942.
37. *Ibid.*
38. *Kigen-setsu*, OM & TNN 11.2.1942.
39. 'One Hundred Million People of Japan Will Celebrate *Tencho-setsu* Today', JT & M 29.4.1942.
40. 'Imperial Birthday', JT & M 29.4.1942.
41. 'Long Live His Majesty the Emperor', OM & TNN 29.4.1942.
42. *Kigen-setsu*, *Nippon Times* (NT) 11.2.1943.
43. *Kigen-setsu*, The *Mainichi* 12.2.1943.
44. *Kigen-setsu*, NT 11.2.1944.
45. 'Strengthen Determination on Each *Kigen-setsu*' The *Mainichi* 12.2.1944.
46. *Tencho-setsu*, NT 29.4.1944.
47. 'Long Live His Majesty the Emperor', The *Mainichi* 29.4.1944.
48. 'Empire's Ideal Must Be Vindicated', The *Mainichi* 12.2.1945.
49. Brown, pp. 92–3.
50. *Tencho-setsu*, NT 29.4.1945.
51. *Ibid.*
52. *Ibid.*
53. 'Long Live His Majesty', The *Mainichi* 29.4.1945.

# 8

# The post-surrender democratisation of Japan: Was it a revolution?

ISONO FUJIKO

IN THE BROAD sense of the word 'revolution', meaning a complete change in the polity of a country, Meiji Ishin (The Meiji Restoration of 1868) may be called a revolution which was staged by an internal initiative, though it was led by a dissatisfied samurai class and eventually conducted under the slogan of 'wa-kon yo-sai' rejecting Western values. On the other hand the post-surrender change in Japan was a 'revolution' in that sovereignty was shifted from the *Tennò* (Emperor) to the people and traditional values were drastically modified, even though it was brought about by a strong external initiative. It is true that the democratisation of Japan was not entirely imposed on the Japanese people by the US Occupation. It meant the removal of militarist dictatorship, the formidable obstacle to liberation for the liberal and progressive elements, who had been ferociously persecuted by the secret police up to the Japanese surrender.

In spite of passive resistance from the conservatives, 'democratisation' became the order of the day. Now, nearly half a century after the surrender, we have to examine whether it was really a revolution of the social structure and popular mentality.For one who lived through the period of the great expectation for a democratic Japan, I have to admit that it was partly an illusion. It is true that direct thought control by the state is no longer possible, and the principles of equality of women cannot be reversed. Nevertheless, I hesitate to boast that the democratisation of Japan has been successful. The change in the Occupation policy from democratisation to anti-communism, one of the unfortunate results of the Cold War, helped the return of many former leaders, some of whom had actually been active collaborationists of the militarist regime as well as staunch anti-communists. At the same time, it was unrealistic to expect that the people, who had received intensive indoctrination in the old values of the Family State with absolute devotion to the *Tennò*, could easily understand what democracy meant. Democracy, with liberalism, had been one of the concepts severely attacked by the former regime as minor forms of communism.

For example, in new school textbooks the abolition of the traditional system of the family, the *Ie Seido*, was described as the 'gloomy feudalistic family', and was contrasted with the 'happy democratic family', illustrated by the smiling father playing with children or the husband helping with the dishes. This kind of presentation created the notion that if the father/husband was kind he was democratic. In this way, democracy was easily confused with paternalism, and the real problems of how independent family members can live in harmony together was almost entirely overlooked.

In fact, this interpretation of democracy was also encouraged by progressive leaders and teachers. Up to the surrender, all who were critical of the government had been lumped together as 'reds'. Liberal and progressive intellectuals tended to be sympathetic to communism, partly because they had a kind of guilt complex towards communists. There had been more communists among those who had stood up to the military regime, defying torture and imprisonment, while most of the liberal intellectuals, though inwardly opposed to the regime, had not been courageous enough to do the same.

Moreover, idealisation of the Soviet Union was still prevalent among the leftists of the world, as the result of the communist resistance to the domination of fascism. In Japan where individualism, in the sense of the right to be different from the others, had been a subversive idea, even the progressives had no particular compunction about the idea of 'following the leader', provided that the leader was supposed to be representing the people. To attain unanimity was considered to be the most democratic process of decision-making.

In this kind of social climate *wa* continued to be the ideal of social relationships, without being subjected to careful scrutiny or analysis. When *wa* is translated as 'harmony', as is usually the case, it sounds quite all right and desirable. In Japan, however, *wa* is a concept very different from harmony. In its original sense in China, the character of *wa* meant almost exactly 'harmony'. In the *Shunju Sashi*

*Den*, a chronicle by a contemporary of Confucius, a cultivated retainer is recorded to have advised his lord (in 522 BC) that *wa* is created when a subject proposes an idea different from that of the lord, and the lord accepts his advice. Amalgamation of different elements gives birth to a new synthesis of a higher quality. Confucius also said '*Wa shite do zezu*' (Harmony, but not conformity).

In Japan, the famous 17 Article Constitution (604 AD) of Shotoku Taishi starts with '*Wa* should be the most precious thing'. But in the following articles subjects are reminded 'not to contradict', and that the lord is as Heaven and the subject as Earth. The booklets, published by the Ministry of Education during the Second World War, are full of instructions as to how to create and maintain *wa*.

1) Each person should know his/her own station in the group to which he belongs.
2) The inferior should obey and serve his superior with self-negating devotion.
3) The superior should recognise the sincerity of the inferior and treat him with benevolence.
4) With this mutual consideration, the members of a group will merge into one indivisible entity and have one mind.

The last point was epitomised in the slogan during the war: 'To embrace the mind of the *Tennō* as one's own mind,' and 'One hundred million (the whole nation) with one mind'. To have different opinions from those of the other members of the group was disapproved of and suppressed because this was seen as disruptive to *wa*.

In the course of democratisation, when the 'feudalistic' family system was criticised as authoritarian and 'dark', its defendants argued that the traditional family was the place where the members lived in the most happy *wa*. The post-surrender confusion in family life caused by the sudden change made the latter statement quite convincing. Many scholars, including Takeyoshi Kawashima, maintained that these two opposing aspects had somehow been combined in the old family system.

It seems to me that these aspects of severity and happy *wa* are not two opposing aspects but two sides of the same coin called *wa*. In the *wa* system, if everyone in the group sticks to the rule without reasoning why, or at least with resignation, the system works quite smoothly; but once one of them wants to have his/her own way that person is placed under strong pressure to conform, and overtly or tacitly censured for having disrupted *wa*; and the head is supposed to exercise his authority to maintain *wa* in the group.

It is not correct, however, to interpret the authority of the head or the superior as a *right* to wield arbitrary power over the inferior. Theoretically it is his duty to be benevolent to the inferior, but if he does not behave as is prescribed, it is only his superior who can chide him for his misdemeanour, and it is only his equal who can advise him to have more consideration for his inferior. Nevertheless, the inferior has no right (a very subversive concept in the system of *wa*) to protest. Even when his conduct or opinion is objectively correct, it is not for him to stand up against his superior. The more injustice he endures and the longer he continues to be obedient, the greater the popular praise and sympathy accorded to his loyalty and perseverance.

In feudal times, the subject sometimes practised *seppuku* to make his lord repent for the unjust treatment of an inferior. Now, an employee has to risk his post or job to do so. *Amae*, made famous by Doi Takeo as the key concept for analysing Japanese society, can be used to influence the superior to modify his attitude. Before the surrender, a woman notable, who gave advice in the advice column of a women's magazine, enjoined an unhappy daughter-in-law to practise *amae* on her mother-in-law to make her more lenient toward her.

In other words, *amae* is an expression of submission to one's superior in the hope of obtaining a favour from the latter. In this context *amaeru* may be translated as 'to ingratiate' or even 'to fawn on'.

Incidentally, it seems to me that it is not so much the concept of *amae* itself but the very permissive attitude to *amae* that is particularly Japanese; and *wa* seems to me to be more cardinal concept to analyse the Japan society than *amae*, which is rather a kind of lubricant to make a hierarchical society of *wa* function smoothly.

In this way *wa* is the cardinal virtue in a hierarchical society with a double standard for the superior and the inferior. Of course, in any society some kind of hierarchy is indispensable to make the system work efficiently. Nevertheless, in Japan the hierarchy of roles in an organisation is inseparable from the hierarchy of the value of the persons occupying different posts (*erai* and *erakunai*). The work hierarchy is directly related to the status hierarchy.

It is often said that Japan is the world's most egalitarian society, giving as examples that in a factory everybody, the workers and directors, wear the same uniform, eat in the same dining hall, and so on. This does not mean at all that the workers can treat their superiors as equals. Attitudes and forms of speech are minutely prescribed in conformity with the grading of status in the enterprise in all social contacts as well as at work.

What is known as the workers' identification with the enterprise to which they belong and so on, is, theoretically, based on the 'individual-less' (not quite the same as 'selfless') devotion of the employees, compensated by the paternalism of the enterprise. The tricky point is that because of the generous welfare benefits, the employees are supposed to be morally obliged not to be ungrateful, and practically tied to the enterprise with material advantages. To have accommodation provided by the company is something not easily discarded when the alternative is a very high rent to be paid for a much smaller flat, often entailing longer commuting time.

One thing should especially be noted concerning the concept of *wa*. It is a general formula used to contrast Western individualism with Japanese groupism. Certainly, *wa* is the thing that makes Japanese merge into a group; but this group does not include those who do not belong to the same '*wa* group'. The outsiders and outside groups are either strangers whom you can neglect, or treat with respectful or disdainful distance according to their recognised superiority or inferiority; or they can be rivals against whom your own group has to struggle for supremacy.

The *wa* group, however, is not a well-defined entity. One *wa* group is subdivided into smaller ones, and their formation is quite flexible according to circumstance, and it can be conceptually expanded to cover the Japanese nation, but not so far as to cover the whole of humanity. This partly explains why the Japanese seem to be so ready to render self-negating devotion to their own group, but so slow in responding to the call for voluntary activities to help handicapped persons, or victims of catastrophes, both natural and political.

Then again the *wa* group is not formed by individuals getting together with solidarity, but formed by the members merging themselves into one entity. Therefore, in a way the group is the expanded self of the members, and the prosperity of the company, or the nation, is felt to be their own prosperity, even though their salaries do not go up in proportion to the profit made by the company. It is true that such an identification with the company makes each employee feel responsible for whatever concerns the company, even when he himself is not the person who was directly responsible for the matter in question, assuring the quality of the products.

There is no doubt that this kind of individual-less merging into the enterprise has greatly contributed to the rapid economic expansion, which has revived confidence in the 'groupism' in contrast to individualism, which has not been differentiated from selfishness. In fact, a very selfish motive of remaining in favour with the superior and evading disapproval of his fellow-workers prevents a man from expressing his personal opinion (except concerning the technical improvement of the products). Here is a renaissance of *wa-kon yo-sai*. *Wa* prevents them from taking the initiative in improving working conditions by organising a group in solidarity with co-workers. The excessive labour movements, in Britain for example, which slowed down the national production, have given encouragement to the principle of 'cooperation of the employers and the employees', based on hard-working employees and paternalistic employers.

Such devotion to the group is, however, partly '*tatemae*' though the mental training from childhood, now more in schools than at home, has cultivated in most of the employees an inhibition to express their '*honne*'. It is only recently that the long working hours and the increasing number of deaths caused by over-work have come to be taken up in public discussion.

Except for public servants, who are in the privileged position of being able to enjoy 20 days of paid vacation, in the private sector, even though employees are legally entitled to have from eight to 20 days of paid holidays a year, (including sick-leave, and starting only from the second year of service), only a very few dare to 'consume' the period of the paid vacation. This is not so much because of direct control from above, but a man who is taking the full period of his legal vacation has told me that his annual salary is far below and his promotion has been much slower than his 'diligent' fellow workers of the same category. The consideration of not causing inconvenience to his fellow-workers (as *tatemae*), and the tacit disapproval of his co-workers (*honne*), as well as the pressure from above, make it difficult for him to profit from his legal right.

It is true that he is not forced to go on working, but in reality he cannot do otherwise. It seems to be typically Japanese that even though there are demands by the family of the victims to have *karō-shi*, death from overwork, recognised as *rosai-shi*, death that was caused by working for the company, there are many fewer organised demands for removing the cause of such deaths by improving working conditions. Now it is the government, partly under the external pressure, that has started to 'give guidance' to shorten working hours and encourage the full consumption of paid vacation. In response to this, some companies, 'with paternal solicitude', are providing facilities and even giving out booklets to show how to enjoy vacations.

Where the idea of fundamental equality of persons is not accepted, except for the letter of the Constitution, 'paternalism' is a virtue, and the word or the concept has no negative connotation. With the revival of confidence in traditional values as the result of economic success, and helped by cultural relativism, individuality and even human rights are sometimes labelled 'Western concepts', which cannot be applied to the Japanese society. A university professor at an international symposium stated that the concept of human rights was a product of the Western society based on contract, and 'one-sided'(?) emphasis on human rights might lead to 'a society where everyone will sue everyone,' and that 'a really peaceful society would be one where the concept of human rights will no longer be necessary.' (Of course, one can argue that no law is necessary when all men become saints.)

It is true that human rights, freedom of conscience and democracy are all products of Western society with the tradition of Christianity; and each nation should be allowed to develop its own cultural heritage. Nevertheless, industrialisation also originated in the West. It seems to me that industrialisation has its own logic. That is to say: if you have adopted industrialisation, unless you accept also the political and economic rules and ethics of an industrialised society, such as the fundamental equality of persons, the right to dissent, and democratic systems to check abuses of power, the weaker section of society will be at the mercy of the stronger, in a more ruthless way than in the pre-industrial society.

Paternalism may protect the weak, but paternalism is left to the arbitrary practice of benevolence by the superior and cannot be claimed by the inferior. If you adopt the system like industrialisation which originated in the West, to stick to the slogan of '*wa-kon yo-sai*' does not seem to be fair (another concept alien to the traditional hierarchical society) to the people without power.

In the West, the legitimacy of protesting against secular political power developed rather early. It seems to me that its origin was not entirely religious but at least partly political. In the struggle for power between the Pope and the King, the Pope gave sanction to the resistance to the secular political power, opening up the way to the legitimacy of freedom of conscience and conscientious objection. In China, while the superior was supposed to practise *jin* (benevolence), even in the case of the Emperor, if he failed to be worthy of his title, Heaven withdrew its sanction from him. *Ge-ming* (*kakumei* in Japanese) is the word used for translating 'revolution'. Its original meaning is 'renovation of the Mandate of Heaven'. The idea is that if the ruler failed to practise *jin* and became oppressive, then Heaven withdrew its mandate from the ruler. The Renovation of the Heavenly mandate was thought to be executed by some revolutionary who overthrew the corrupt dynasty. Even though Chinese peasants were actually helpless in the hands of the landlords, the legitimacy to protect against abuse of power was there.

Japan has prided itself for never having had a revolution, and the line of the *Tennō* is supposed to have continued right from the beginning. In reality, there were a number of *Tennō* deposed or exiled; but, except for the legendary attempt of Dokyo to usurp the throne of the *Tennō* (in mid 760s), all shoguns who came into power preferred to use the *Tennō* as the emblem of legitimacy for them to wield political power. The Meiji Government fully utilised this system by making the *Tennō* sacrosanct, so that anything done by the government, in the name of the *Tennō*, was above criticism, let alone protest. Without the tradition of 'Renovation of Heavenly Mandate' there has been no firm ground for legitimacy in protesting against the abuse of power, and in asserting the justifiable rights of individuals.

Even though the post-surrender New Constitution gave sovereignty to the people represented by the Diet, the very fact of having had the Imperial Diet since 1890 seems to have blurred the real significance of the revolutionary change. Those who have been elected immediately become 'sensei', and voters are still very much influenced by personal connections rather than the policy advocated by the candidates. The procedure of election itself is sometimes felt as something to 'disrupt wa and leave an awkward aftermath.'

This may be an extremely simplistic statement, but unless wa will become 'harmony' and not 'unison', the real transformation of Japanese subjects into modern citizens, namely a revolution of mentality, seems to be still far away. It is easy to say we must preserve good tradition and discard undesirable elements. Nevertheless, every merit has its own demerit. It is not easy to change a structure which has developed over centuries. What should be explored may not be a choice between individualism and groupism, or proposals for an easy-going amalgamation. In the world where no nation can be isolationist and all nations have to share certain fundamental values to be able to work together, the most important task is to develop a new way of life in which independent individuals can work in harmony, through free exchange of ideas with the aim of securing fundamental human rights for an ever increasing number of the world population.

**9**

# A revolution in labour law? The fate of the trade union act in post-war Japan

ANTHONY WOODIWISS

IT IS OFTEN and correctly maintained that the passage of the post-war Trade Union Act initiated a revolution in Japanese industrial relations. It is not so often recognised that the persistence of certain social-structural continuities between pre- and post-war Japan has led to the partial reversal of this revolution. Drawing on my recent book-length study (Woodiwiss, 1992), the present paper specifies the nature of this reversal in the course of an examination of the most important labour law cases of the post-war period.

My specific thesis is that the prime reason for this reversal has been that, because of the society's post-war economic success, it has proved possible to 'reinvent' Japan's traditional ideology – to reinvent it in the form of a largely secular and sociologised ideological formation which I have termed *Kigyōshugi* or 'enterprisism'. This is a formation wherein belief in the intrinsic virtue of the company as the most significant contemporary instance of the traditional and supposedly unique *ie* (patriarchal household) form of social organisation has been replaced by pre-war belief in the intrinsic virtue of the *Tennō*. It is also a formation that for similar patriarchalist reasons continues *Tennōsei*'s hostility towards fully autonomous and assertive trade unions.

In what follows I will suggest, first, that the statutes upon which the post-war labour law system was based may be read as instances of a fundamental ideological continuity between pre- and post-war Japan; and second that the reason why labour law has latterly become at least as much of a hindrance as a help to trade unions is because, given its intrinsic patriarchalism it has proved to be highly susceptible to *Kigyōshugi*-inspired interpretations on the part of the

116

Judiciary – interpretations which have resulted in these continuities becoming ever more marked with the passage of time. The result of the latter movement is that it has reduced still further labour law's anyway inherently limited capacity to serve as a means for the enforcement of a certain democratism in the workplace. In sum, then, what I intend to specify here is the concrete nature of *Kigyōshugi* in a particular sphere.

Although it has seldom been fully acknowledged in the relevant literature, the same ambiguity as to what it might signify (i.e. democratism or patriarchalism) characterised even the amended Trade Union Law of 1949 as, on my reading at least, characterised the 'New Constitution'. On the one hand, the passage of the law, like the presence of labour rights in the constitution, undoubtedly granted labour in both the private and public sectors rights a degree of social recognition which it had never possessed before (only the police, firefighters and prison staff were excluded from this dispensation). On the other hand, it did so on the basis of a bill which, highly suggestively and as Sheldon Garon (1987) has recently pointed out, had first been prepared by the Home Ministry's Social Bureau in 1925.

Also passed into law during the early days of the Occupation were two other labour laws which, although this has been commented upon even less often, similarly owed much to pre-war state patriarchalism, the Labour Relations Adjustment Act (LRAA) of 1946, the Labour Standards Act of 1947, and the Public Corporation and National Enterprise Labour Relations Law (PCLL) of 1948. I do not intend to attempt to justify my reading of the basic texts here since I have done this at some length in my book. Suffice it to say that throughout the legislation the fact that labour rights were granted for a purpose rather than for the sake of a principle is made very explicit (i.e. they were granted in order to enable trade unions to fit into a surprisingly pre-systematised framework of industrial relations rather than to enable employees to contribute to the construction of a such a system). Anyway, instead of saying anything further by way of justification, I will proceed more or less immediately to a presentation of the judicial interpretations of the same texts – interpretations which make it clear that, especially after 1972, the majority of Supreme Court Justices may be read as having supported my claim, albeit whilst placing an opposite and positive valuation upon it.

I say 'especially after 1972' not so much because during the preceding two years the make-up of the Supreme Court was transformed by the arrival of seven new and very conservative Justices, but more because *Kigyōshugi* was hegemonically established by that time and so readily available for enunciation by such Justices.

Ideally, in a civil law system such as Japan's, case law and even the judgements of the Supreme Court should be of little consequence. In reality, of course, the proliferation of subsidiary and/or related statutes and changing social conditions more generally mean that divergent interpretations of the law amongst both legal practitioners and interested parties become ever more likely and that authoritative interpretations become increasingly necessary. Post-war Japan has proved to be no exception to this rule, except that because of union poverty, the expensiveness of legal proceedings and the pre-emptive effects of *Kigyōshugi*, the courts have had and, what is perhaps even more to the point, have taken far fewer opportunities to set out their interpretations than in comparable European legal systems.

Of the reasons just given for the relative paucity of Japan's case law, one is by far the most important, namely the preemptive effects of *Kigyōshugi*. Not only does the presence of this discourse in the workplace dramatically reduce the likelihood of such disputes becoming public in the first place, but because of its insistence on the preferability of conciliation, it also reduces the likelihood of them providing grist for the juridical mill.

The result is that most of even the few disputes that become public and which have the potential to be legally interesting come before the Labour Commissions, who typically conciliate them and so deprive them of any legal significance as regards the specification of the rights and duties of the parties involved. Moreover, the courts too would appear to prefer that even the disputes that are brought to them are conciliated rather than decided, since they often encourage 'out-of-court' settlements even in mid-trial. In this way, then, the law has been pre-empted, avoided and thus, to a degree derogated. It should come as no surprise, therefore, that, with a few minor and/or transitory exceptions, even when it has been invoked labour law has contributed to the gradual establishment of

*Kigyōshugi*'s hegemony within Japanese workplaces. This said, a reading of the case law nevertheless provides plenty of evidence that Japanese workplaces remain far less harmonious places in fact than they are commonly pictured to be, as well as some that suggest that it remains a possibility, albeit an extremely unlikely one, that labour law may yet be made to reinforce discourses other than *Kigyōshugi*. Here I have in mind a series of recent decisions that have belatedly addressed the issue of intra-union democracy.

Anyway, turning to my history of the case law, no sooner had the amendments to the Trade Union Law been passed than the Supreme Court was asked in the case of Okada v. Japan (1950) to consider the legality of a sit-down or 'production control' strike in which the strikers had not only continued production but had also sold some of the products of their labour in order to meet their wage and other bills (Maki, 1964, pp. 274–81). For this the strike leaders were arrested, tried and found guilty of the theft of company property. I will not dwell on the significance of this result except to say that, in finding the strikers guilty, the Court provided a benchmark against which to judge the ideological movement of post-war labour law.

In other words, the post-war judicial history of Japan's labour law begins with what was for Japan an unparalledly powerful assertion of capital's privileged position in society and, because of this, in the law too. It therefore suggests that at least initially a rather different conception of the nature of Japanese enterprises informed labour law as compared to that propagated by *Kigyōshugi*. This initial conception was one that stressed the conflicting interests of capital and labour and which, given that it was enunciated in a democratic context, might therefore have been expected to have led the judiciary to have been as concerned to protect the interests of labour as those of capital.

Although the Court did not make the point explicitly, one of the principles upon which it based itself was the rider added to Article 12 of the New Constitution to the effect that 'the people . . . shall refrain from any abuse of these freedoms and rights and shall always be responsible for using them in the public welfare' (this article was, however, listed first amongst the Court's references).

The relativising of the people's rights and freedoms was a theme that the Court returned to, this time explicitly, in its next significant labour law case, which I will call the Tokyo Electric Express Railway Company Case. This was a case which came before the Court in 1951 and related to circumstances where several employees of a railway company provided stories to Communist party newspapers which alleged corruption in the relations between the company and the union. The company invoked its disciplinary regulations and dismissed the authors of the stories for slandering the company and hindering its efficient operations. In response the dismissed workers sued for reinstatement on the grounds that their rights to freedom of expression, as well as their trade union rights, had been violated. The Court's dismissal of this argument centred on the free speech issue and largely concurred with the judgement of the lower court that:

> The act of publication carried out under Article 21 [the free speech clause, A.W.] *naturally* cannot be interpreted as having been guaranteed without any attendant responsibilities. Accordingly, persons who engage in such acts of publication must inevitably find themselves in a position in which they are responsible under both criminal and civil law for such acts . . . When the conduct of the appellants . . . came under the disciplinary regulations of the said company, then a situation arose that *naturally* and necessarily had to be dealt with by the said company in accordance with the . . . regulations and it is impossible to construe Article 21 of the Constitution as having any effect on the validity of the above disciplinary regulations. [my italics]

What is particularly interesting about this judgement, apart from its substantive content, is the confident way in which the term 'naturally' is used, especially since it is used in the context of a judgement that sounds far from natural to liberal-democratic ears and perhaps especially to American ones. My suggestion is that what allowed this confidence was an unspoken, background assumption as to how things should be in a Japanese enterprise, which assumption corresponds to the patriarchalist *ie* ideal. This ideal was, then, able to enter legal discourse thanks to the Court's insistence that constitutional freedoms were not absolute and could be qualified either in the light of Court determined considerations of the public welfare or because of 'obligations freely contracted'. This case therefore represents the founding moment of *Kigyōshugi* as far as labour law is concerned – employee rights are not only subordinate to those of the employer but also do not enjoy the same judicially protected status.

Moving on through the case law more rapidly now, throughout the 1950s, the various issues prompted by the restrictions on the rights of public sector employees bubbled beneath the surface as time and again they went on strike in defiance of these restrictions. Since the issues raised by the cases that resulted are the best-known aspects of Japan's post-war labour law history, I will say nothing about them here although they are discussed at length in my book-length study. Suffice it to say on this occasion that the severe restrictions imposed upon public sector unions, especially their lack of the right to strike, were by and large confirmed as constitutional.

The clearest evidence for the proposition that the Trade Union Act, as interpreted by the judiciary, has facilitated the spread of *Kigyōshugi* in private workplaces, may be provided by: 1) a consideration of the legal tolerance afforded joint consultation and the uses to which such consultation has been put; and 2) a consideration of the reasoning behind the restrictions that have been imposed on 'acts of dispute' since the early 1970s.

In the United States the existence of the National Labour Relations Act's insistence on union autonomy, as specified in its unfair labour practice provisions, has led to the judicial imposition of rather strict limits on union–management cooperation. It would appear that the existence of a very similar set of provisions in the Trade Union Act has had no such result. This suggests that the Japanese judiciary has read these provisions in the context of a rather different set of non-juridical discourses to those which have informed the readings provided by their American opposite numbers. More specifically, it suggests that the Japanese judiciary has read these provisions in the light of *Kigyōshugi* with its preference for 'harmony', rather than in the light of the American preference for the clear differentiation of management and labour rights (Woodiwiss, 1990, ch. 8).

In the same way that it may be argued that the American courts' response had had negative consequences in relation to the improvement of the relations between labour and capital (Gould, 1984, pp. 165–5), so it may also be argued that the Japanese courts have failed to indicate much sensitivity to the complexities involved in the notion of industrial democracy. To support this proposition, I will simply point out the following: first, that the joint consultation for which most unions have sacrificed much of their autonomy very seldom takes the form of bargaining; second, that when it does take the form of bargaining (e.g. in relation to transfers, redundancy and retirement), it is much more likely to involve issues of employee discipline than other management actions such as 'basic production and sales plans'; third, that unions are almost always at a disadvantage in any such bargaining, because the sorts of issues it is most likely to relate to are generally those covered by the company 'works rules', which all employees have already acceded to as a condition of employment; and, finally, that authoritative case commentary also makes it clear that not even consultative agreements, let alone any 'understandings' that might have been arrived at as regards the negotiability of such rules, are necessarily accepted as binding by the courts.

Joint consultation, therefore, is better understood as a means of gaining union support for a company's disciplinary structure *vis à vis* its employees than as a means whereby a measure of industrial democracy is brought to the workplace. This is a point that gains still greater force once it is realised: first, that legally the collective agreement takes precedence over the individual contract of employment, even when the terms of the former are not as good as those of the latter (Hanami, 1979, p. 113; for English moves in this direction, see Leader, 1989); and second, that grievance procedures which include the possibility of outside arbitration are virtually unknown in Japanese workplaces (Sugeno, nd. p. 14.).

The topic whose discussion would best illustrate this point would be that of *shukkō* (transfers to related firms), which is the point at which the paternalist obligation to provide 'lifetime employment' comes into conflict with as well as contributes to the supposed harmony of the Japanese workplace. All that will be said on this occasion is that 30 years ago transfers were very seldom challenged (Hanami, 1979, p. 60), but today, when something like 6 to 8 per cent of employees are transferred every year, they are contested surprisingly often, which results in unions being placed in what one might suppose would be a very uncomfortable position, especially if transfers are among the issues about which they consult and/or bargain. That is, the burden very often falls on them to try to convince the aggrieved individual that they should accept the transfer on pain of a dismissal that the union may not be willing or able to challenge; see Toppan Insatsu Disciplinary Dismissal Incident, 1957. Thus, alongside the maintenance of a dual labour market and the institutionalisation of the temporary worker system, the enforcement of *shukkō* is one of the principal ways in which employees have been made to play their part in the attainment of Japan's renowned flexibility.

Turning now to the way in which the meaning of the phrase 'acts of dispute' has been restricted, because of the importance of works rules and joint consultation, collective agreements in Japan, especially in comparison to the United States, tend to be very vague documents concerned only with the broadest of generalities. The somewhat ironic and, from the point of view of the trade unions, the beneficent result is that, although the Japanese courts have read into such agreements the assumption of 'a peace obligation' by both parties for the duration of the contract, in another rather stark contrast to what happens in the United States they have very seldom found striking unions to be in breach of such an obligation even though employers have often asked the courts to try.

Less surprisingly, because it derives directly from the constitutional protection given to collective bargaining as well as from the broad definitions of an 'act of dispute' contained in the Labour Relations Adjustment Law, Japanese unions also appear to enjoy a greater tactical freedom as to the means they may use to pursue their ends than their American and European counterparts. Moreover, as Hanami (1979, pp. 119, 130) notes, their right to use the various 'acts of dispute' at their disposal is stronger than the employers' right to resort to lockouts, since the latter does not enjoy constitutional protection.

All that said, there are nevertheless significant restrictions on the right to strike. These derive from the close legislative specification of the purposes for which the right to engage in 'acts of dispute' may be used. On this basis the courts have typically found that a very broadly defined category of 'political' strikes etc. do not enjoy any greater legal protection in private industry than they do in the public sector. In addition, and more interestingly because this is an instance of the judicial discovery of 'unfair labour practices' on labour's part that scholars such as Hanami have claimed do not exist, the courts have typically found that 'sympathy strikes' too are unprotected.

Now, one great disadvantage suffered by enterprise unions, as contrasted to the national craft and/or industrial unions more typical of other societies, is their inability to build up substantial strike funds. For this reason Japanese strikes tend to be very short. As well as not finding their way into the strike statistics which only include strikes of longer than four hours, their place as the 'act of dispute' is very often taken by such activities as picketing, working to rule, coordinated holiday taking, pasting posters and, most distinctively, wearing ribbons that specify not only the reasons for disputes but also the protesting employees opinions of their employers. Because of this, any judgement as to the significance that should be attached to any latitude that employees have been granted in the use that they can make of such acts has to bear in mind that the unions depend upon them as surrogates for strike action.

Until the early 1970s, both the Labour Commissions and the courts tended to show greater toleration of such activities and indeed of violence than was the case, for example, in the United States (Fukui, 1973). This is no longer the case today. As in the case of the rights of public sector unions, the period since the early 1970s has seen a tightening-up of the restrictions on the 'acts of dispute' allowed to private sector unions. For example and again inspired by ideas as the sorts of behaviour that are proper in *Japanese* companies, the courts have made it clear that any violence on a union's part will result not simply in criminal charges but also in an immediate loss of standing before the courts (Kotobuki Architectural Research Company Case, 1977).

Similarly, the courts have also shown themselves to be less tolerant than they used to be as regards 'ribbon struggles'. When the Tokyo Local Labour Relations Commission first considered the matter in the Hotel Okura Case (1972), it allowed that when a dispute was in progress the works rules were suspended and so it found nothing wrong with the staff's wearing of ribbons critical of the management. By contrast, when the Tokyo District Court considered the same case on appeal in 1975, it found that 'ribbon struggles were illegal in general'. The court's reasoning is particularly interesting in the present context, since its dependence on the discourse of *Kigyōshugi* is very clear.

For this reason I have quoted from and discussed the judgement at some length in my book (see pp. 135–6). In the present context I will only quote that part of the judgement where the court explains why the practice of ribbon struggles is bad for employees as well as employers:

> '[it creates] a psychological dual structure which on the one hand is obedient and on the other is antagonistic towards superiors and [so] divides the psychological operations of people who are logical beings, paving the way for the formation of split personalities.'

On this reasoning, then, ongoing face-to-face disagreement with one's superior is likely to lead to schizophrenia – of course it is not, but what it does do is violate the *ie* ideal. In 1982 the Tokyo Labour Commission appealed the case to the Supreme Court on behalf of the union concerned. The Supreme Court upheld both the judgement and the amateur psychological reasoning of the lower court.

In sum, then, prompted by a conciliatory methodology for dealing with conflicts over rights that Beer (1968) has appropriately termed 'harmonising' to distinguish it from the 'balancing' performed by American judges, the Japanese Supreme Court has depended upon *Kigyōshugi*-inspired ideas to weaken trade unions in the following ways: by preferring conciliation to arbitration as well as adjudication; by allowing that constitutional freedoms may be negotiated away in the case of 'contracts that have been freely entered into'; by reasserting the constitutionality of hitherto suspect restrictions on the right to strike in the public sector; by allowing the legality of joint consultation arrangements that grievously threaten the independence of trade unions, despite the existence of the same unfair labour practice provisions that disallow such arrangements in the United States; by making involuntary overtime as well as transfers to so-called 'related companies' irresistible by individual employees; and finally by making 'ribbon struggles' illegal.

To conclude, the patriarchalism intrinsic to *Kigyōshugi* has both ensured the constitutionality of some of the more questionable statutory articles (here I have in mind particularly the restrictions on the rights of public sector unions), and more importantly in the light of the privatisations of the 1980s, it has also transformed the conception of the employment relationship in the private sector that was basic to both the New Constitution and the amended Trade Union Law; i.e. the recognition of the different interests of capital and labour that was fundamental to the post-war legislation has been ever more confidently denied as social and judicial commitment to the hollow communitarianism of the company has grown. What, I wonder, will be the effect, if any, of the recent exposees of systematic corruption within the corporate sector on the popular belief in the intrinsic virtue of the company that reflects and underpins these commitments?

## BIBLIOGRAPHY

AYUSAWA, I. (1966) *A History of Labour in Modern Japan*, East West Center Press, Honolulu.
BEER, L. (1968) 'The Public Welfare Standard and Freedom of Expression in Japan', in Henderson (1968).
FUKUI, T. (1973) 'Labour–Management Relations in Japan (II): Acts of Dispute', *Sophia University Socio-Economic Institute Bulletin*, No. 50.
GARON, S. (1987)*The State and Labour in Modern Japan*, University of California Press, Berkeley.
GOULD, W. (1984) *Japan's Reshaping of American Labour Law*, MIT Press, Cambridge, Mass.
HANAMI, T. (1979) *Labour Law and Industrial Relations in Japan*, Kluwer, Deventer.
HANAMI, T., BLANPAIN, R. (eds) (1989) *Industrial Conflict Resolution in Market Societies* , Kluwer, Deventer.
HARARI, E., (1973) *The Politics of Labour Legislation*, University of California Press, Berkeley.
HENDERSON, D.F. (ed.) (1968) *The Constitution of Japan: Its First Twenty Years*, University of Washington Press, Seattle.
ITOH,, H., BEER, L. (eds) (1978) *The Constitutional Case Law of Japan: Selected Supreme Court Decisions, 1961–79*, University of Washington Press, Seattle.
Japan Institute of Labour (1983) *Highlights in Japanese Industrial Relations*, Vol. 1, Tokyo.
Japan Institute of Labour (1988) *Highlights in Japanese Industrial Relations*, Vol. 2, Tokyo.
KOMIYA, F. (1986) 'A Comparative Analysis of the Law of Dismissal in Great Britain, Japan and the USA', ST/ICERD Discussion Paper, London School of Economics.
KUWAHARA, Y. (1989) *The Industrial Relations System in Japan: A New Interpretation*, The Japan Institute of Labour, Tokyo.
MAKI, J. (ed.) (1964) *Court and Constitution in Japan*, University of Washington Press, Seattle.
OHTA, T. (1988) 'Works Rules in Japan', *International Labour Review*, Vol. 127, No. 5, pp. 627–39.

OPPLER, A.C. (1976) *Legal Reform in Occupied Japan: A Participant Looks Back*, Princeton University Press, Princeton, New Jersey.

SUGENO, K. (1989) '*Sbukkō*: An Aspect of the Changing Labour Market in Japan', *Japan Labour Bulletin*, Vol. 28, No. 4.

SUGENO, K. (no date) 'Resolution of Shop Floor Disputes in Japan', mimeo, Faculty of Law, University of Tokyo.

SUGENO, K. (1979) 'Public Employee Strike Problem and its Legal Regulation in Japan', *Current Studies in Japanese Law*, Centre for Japanese Studies, University of Michigan, Ann Arbor.

SUGIMOTO, Y., SHIMADA, H., LEVINE, S. (1982) *Industrial Relations in Japan*, Japanese Studies Centre, Melbourne.

SUWA, Y. (1989) 'Unfair Labour Practices Involving JR Firms', *Japan Labour Bulletin*, Vol. 28, No. 11.

WOODIWISS, A. (1990a) *Rights v. Conspiracy: A Sociological Essay on the History of Labour Law in the United States*, Berg, Oxford.

WOODIWISS, A. (1992) *Labour and Society in Japan: From Repression to Reluctant Tolerance*, Routledge, London.

127

10

# Japanese perceptions of the 1989 Eastern European revolutions*

KATŌ TETSURO

## THE EAST EUROPEAN REVOLUTIONS IN WORLD HISTORY

THE GREAT political change in the Eastern European countries in 1989 has shaken contemporary international relations. This change has a global historical significance. It started in Poland, spread to Hungary, Bulgaria, East Germany, Czechoslovakia and Romania, overthrew communist one-party dictatorships, and achieved democratisation. It demonstrated the vitality of liberty and democracy, destroyed the Berlin Wall, led to the end of the Cold War, and created a new European order. It came in reaction to Gorbachev's *perestoroika*, one of the preconditions for the change, and brought about a multi-party system and a presidential system in the then Soviet Union. It shocked the actually existing socialist countries and international communist movement, led to changes of government in Yugoslavia, Albania and Mongolia as well as the democratisation of African socialism, and effected the conversion of the Italian Communist Party into the Left Democratic Party.

We cannot yet foresee the final results of these political changes. But East Germany has already been absorbed into West Germany. Poland, Hungary, Czechoslovakia and Romania have introduced market economies and the stock-company system. Even the former Soviet Union,

* This paper was written for my presentation to the 7th National Conference of the Japanese Studies Association of Australia, 11–13 July 1991, The Australian National University, Canberra, and to the 6th Triennial International Conference of the European Association for Japanese Studies (EAJS), 16–19 September 1991, Berlin. It first appeared as an article in the Hitotsubashi Journal of Social Studies 23 (1991) 1–23. The author would like to thank Dr Andrew Gordon of Duke University, USA, for his helpful comments and editorial assistance with the English.

suffering from economic crisis and ethnic conflict, depends on foreign aid. The former socialist bloc is being reabsorbed into the capitalist world system. The Warsaw Military Pact has already been dissolved.

Thus, the socialist system actually existing since 1917 has surely entered a period of decline. International communist movements that originated with the Comintern (1919–43) in Lenin's time are facing a crisis of dissolution and collapse. Communist and socialist ideology are losing their attraction. Not only liberalism, democracy and the market mechanism but also even capitalism has gained a better image.

In my Japanese book, *The Eastern European Revolution and Socialism* (Kodansha, Tokyo, March 1990), I summarised the meaning of these political changes as follows:

> 'The linked political revolutions of 1989 through "forum and round table" in Eastern European countries were democratic revolutions which recovered the basic ideas of the 1789 French Revolution. They were civil revolutions in which ordinary people played the decisive role. The scale and impact can be compared with the 1848 Western European Revolution.
>
> The revolutions overthrew the so-called dictatorship of the proletariat and the political rule by a monolithic vanguard party which has been carried on by the communist parties created by Lenin and developed by the Comintern. They signalled the beginning of the historical collapse of the state socialism that originated in Lenin's *The State and Revolution* and in the 1917 Russian Revolution itself.
>
> These revolutions marked a new state in "the reabsorption of state power by society", an ideal that grew up from early socialist thought and that Marx found in the 1871 Paris Commune (*The Civil War in France*). They constitute a part of a worldwide "permanent democratic revolution" that is taking place in the shadow of the nuclear threat and ecological crisis within the capitalist world system dominated by transnational corporations.'

When I published my recent book, *The Crisis of Socialism and the Rebirth of Democracy* (Kyoiku-Shiryo-Shuppankai, Tokyo, July 1990), I raised for theoretical debate the following three questions concerning the 1989 revolutions:

(1)  Should they be called revolution, reform or counter-revolution?
(2)  What was the main cause of the collapse of Soviet-type socialism? Did the roots lie in the failure of Stalin? Did they originate from Lenin? Or should we trace them back to Marx's theory?
(3)  Where are these revolutions headed? Back to capitalism? Toward a rebirth of socialism and communism? Or some third way?

This paper will examine Japanese reactions to the Eastern European Revolution, including my own. I will discuss these reactions first in relation to the image of revolution in Japan, second in terms of the party politics, and third in relation to the discussion in academic and business circles and mass perception.

## REVOLUTION, REFORM OR COUNTER-REVOLUTION?
## – FROM *ASAHI-SHINBUN* NEWS REPORTS

At the beginning of December 1989 a major international symposium was held under the sponsorship of the West German newspaper *Die Zeit*. The subject was 'Causes and Results of the 1989 Eastern European Revolution'. At the opening session, Professor Ralf Dahrendorf of Oxford spoke about three main issues of the revolution, namely, democracy, the market, and pluralism. He asked as the chair whether we could draw the conclusion that an era of post-communism had arrived. Twenty-five well-known intellectuals and politicians from Europe and the USA were present. These included Daniel Bell, Henry Kissinger, Willy Brandt, Helmut Schmidt, Richard von Weizächer, Iring Fetscher, Oleg Rogomolow, André Fontaine, Sergio Segre, Kjell-Olof Feldt, Jürgen Kuczynski, etc. Of these 25, only Professor Kuczynski, a representative of East Germany, confessed a belief that his country was facing a 'conservative revolution' in a negative sense, if not a 'counter-revolution'. But even though the Ceausescu dictatorship in Romania was still in power at the time, he could not deny the reality of a 'revolution in socialism' (*Die Zeit*, Nr. 1, 20 December 1989).

In January 1990, in his State of the Union address, President Bush in the USA proclaimed the beginning of the new period of world history as a consequence of 'the 1989 revolution in Eastern Europe', and he proposed a new initiative of disarmament in Europe. For people in Europe or the USA, it might be natural that this series of political changes was seen as 'a series of revolutions', variously called a 'self-controlled revolution' in Poland, 'a peaceful revolution' in Hungary, a 'people's revolution' in East Germany, a 'velvet revolution' in Czechoslovakia and an 'anti-communist revolution in Romania. In the East Asian economic giant, Japan, however, it remained a controversial question whether these historical changes should be characterised as 'revolution'. To understand this point, it is interesting how the *Asahi-shinbun*, a representative and high quality Japanese newspaper, described the process of change in Eastern Europe in 1989.

The round table talks between the Polish Workers' Party and Solidarity from February through April, the first free election in June, and the birth of a non-communist cabinet led by Tadeusz Mazowieski in August, were described by the *Asahi-shinbun* as 'reform' or 'democratisation'. The Japanese word 'reform (*kaikaku*)' had already been used as a translation of the Russian word *perestroika*. 'Democratisation (*minshuka*)' was a popular expression for the Chinese student movement from April to 4 June, and the invasion of Tiananmen Square by troops was described as 'the breakdown of democratisation'.

The rise of reformist groups within the Hungarian Socialist Workers' Party, the opening of the border with Austria, the renaming of the Socialist Workers' Party to 'Socialist Party' and of the 'People's Republic' to the 'Republic of Hungary', were also labelled 'reforms'. The dismissal of political leaders in Bulgaria and East Germany were said to be 'changes of government (*seiben*)'. Further, the *Asahi* described the rapid process from the fall of the Berlin Wall and the people's mass movements against the Socialist Unity Party in East Germany to the emergence of President Havel in Czechoslovakia, as a 'transformation (*henkaku*)', 'upheaval (*gekiben*)', and 'convulsion (*gekidō*)', as well as a 'reform' and 'democratisation'.

Only after the collapse of the Romanian Ceausescu dictatorship, did the *Asahi-shinbun* finally use the word 'revolution (*kakumei*)' in a headline.

On 23 December, Yoshio Murakami, the chief foreign news editor of the *Asahi-shinbun*, wrote a column titled, 'The Achievement of the Eastern European Revolution'. On 27 December, the *Asahi* ran an article on 'The Public TV

Station that supported the Romanian Revolution'. The first headline of a 1990 New Year series of articles on 'The Changing World', was 'A New Stage of the Eastern European Revolution'. A headline of 5 January was 'Two Weeks after the Romanian Revolution'.

But the term 'revolution' did not become established on the pages of *Asahi-shinbun*. In subsequent months, the *Asahi* again described the 1990 process of free elections, the setting up of non-communist governments, the introduction of the market economy and foreign investment, or the unification of Germany, as 'reform', 'democratisation', or 'liberation'.

The headline of 'The Second Revolution in the Soviet Union' in February referring to the introduction of a multi-party and president system, was an exception. Also exceptional were two books from the *Asahi-shinbun* publishing house. One was *History Speed Up: From the sites of the Eastern European Revolution* written by a correspondent, *Itoh Chihiro* in June. The other was a collection of newspaper articles entitled *Revolution: A Scenario for the Rebirth of the Soviet Union and East Europe* in October 1990. More typical was the symposium of Eastern European journalists and Japanese scholars organised by the *Asahi-shinbun* in April 1990, named 'The Destination of Eastern European Reforms'. Another representative Japanese newspaper, the *Yomiuri-shinbun*, also arranged an international symposium in April entitled 'The Search for a New World Order: Ramifications of the Soviet and Eastern European Transformation'.

## THE POPULAR IMAGE OF 'REVOLUTION' IN JAPAN – VIOLENT AND BLOODY MASS REVOLT

Why did the expression 'revolution' appear on the pages of the *Asahi-shinbun* only after Romania's Ceausescu government collapsed? The answer probably is related to the image of the word 'revolution' in Japan, the presence of violence and blood in Romania's transformation, and concern for the 'safety of Japanese abroad'.

After the fall of the Berlin Wall and the Malta meeting, the Ceausescu government was seen to be the last dictatorship in Eastern Europe, and for this reason, Japanese people strongly expected it to collapse. After the renaming of the Hungarian Republic in October, Japanese TV news and

132

newspapers often showed maps of 'a wave of democratisation in Eastern Europe'. This became a reality, as expected, just at Christmas time. There were reports of the 'Massacre in Timisoara', 'Gun-shooting, against street demonstration', 'Bloody disaster', and then, the 'Execution of Ceausescu'.

Additionally, there were also reports of the emergency measures committee in the Ministry of Foreign Affairs for the safety of Japanese in Romania, bulletins that a Japanese correspondent was injured, or that 68 Japanese safely fled from Romania to Bulgaria (all above from the headlines of the *Asahi-shinbun* in December 1989). It is well known that the Japanese mass-media tend to focus only on the safety of Japanese when hijackings, airplane accidents or acts of international terrorism occur. Japanese media reacted to the Romanian revolution as it does in these cases. The Romanian TV scenes looked thrilling to many Japanese, just like the Tiananmen Square incidents in June.

But why did the expression 'revolution' fail to become established thereafter on the pages of Japanese newspapers?

In the literature of the UK, USA or France, 'revolution' has a close connection with a historical tradition of people's self-emancipation. There are many studies on these revolutions written in a positive tone. An academic field of 'comparative revolutions' even exists in the West. In Japan, there is no such tradition of 'revolution'. Japanese people have no firm experience of self-emancipation achieved by themselves.

The well-known political change in 1868 in Japan resulted in a great transformation of society similar to the 'revolutions' in Western countries, but this was named the 'Meiji Restoration (*Ishin*)'. Both of the Japanese words *'Ishin* (restoration)' and *'kakumei* (revolution)' originate from Chinese. *'Ishin'* means 'all things are changed and renewed'. The original meaning of *kakumei* was 'the change of Chinese dynasty by fate' or 'great changes' (*ekisei kakumei*), and the meaning shifted to the equivalent of the Western word 'revolution' only after the Meiji period, and now has become established as a translation of 'revolution'. Both words originally had no meaning of self-emancipation or a subjective, active transformation of society by the people (my interpretation of *kakumei* is in *Encyclopedia Nipponica 2001*, Vol. 5, Shogakukan, Tokyo, 1985).

The Meiji upheaval was explained rather as a restoration of the Imperial *Tennō* family than as a great social change, and the people's activity under the leadership of the lower samurai class was rendered as minimal. By calling it the 'Meiji Restoration', the greatest social change in Japanese history was connected with the myth of the long tradition of the *Tennō* regime, and was ideologically separated from such concurrent transformations in the mid-nineteenth century world as the 1848 Western European Revolution, the 1853 Taiping revolt in China, the 1861 Civil War in the US, the 1867 second reform of election system in Britain, the 1871 Paris Commune in France, and the 1870 Italian and the 1871 German state-building.

The transformation from the Imperial system to the contemporary system in 1945 was not a 'revolution from below' but a 'reform from above', forced by the defeat of the Second World War and the US occupation, although one constitutional scholar at the time called it 'the August Revolution'. Thus, Japanese people have experienced great social transformation and moved from the periphery to the core within the capitalist world system without a political 'revolution' in which they took part. They have no positive or subjective image of 'revolution'.

Rather, the image of 'revolution' in modern Japan was strongly determined by the 1789 French Revolution and the 1917 Russian Revolution. The common characteristics as perceived by the Japanese were the great transformation of the social system in a violent and bloody conflict, and mass revolt with the rapid collapse of the existing order. The fact that the *Asahi-shinbun* perceived a 'revolution' only in Romania might come from this traditional image in Japan.

## THE DOMINANT IMAGE OF 'REVOLUTION' IN JAPANESE ACADEMIC CIRCLES – FROM 'BOURGEOIS DEMOCRATIC' TO 'PROLETARIAN SOCIALIST' REVOLUTION

Although a tradition of popular political movement is weak, the intellectual influence of Marxism in academic circles has been strong. Many Japanese Marxists are supportive of socialism due to the long-standing importation of a soviet-type Marxism–Leninism rooted in the Comintern. They wish to build a socialist state and a communist society. They tend to idealise 'revolution' as the only way to reach a Japanese Utopia.

The dominant image of 'revolution' among Japanese intellectuals was either the 'bourgeois democratic revolution' as in 1789 France or the 'proletarian socialist revolution' as in 1917 Russia. These were defined as, first, 'a political revolution as a change in the class character of state power', and secondly, 'a social revolution as a transformation of the economic social formation from feudalism to capitalism or from capitalism to socialism' in an orthodox Marxist sense.

From these dominant, orthodox Marxist viewpoints, Japanese academics believed, on the one hand, in the existence of pre-modern or feudal remnants even in post-war advanced capitalist Japan because of the lack of a 'bourgeois democratic revolution' in history, and on the other, they held sacred the actually existing socialism such as that of the Soviet Union or the People's Republic of China for the reason that these countries had already achieved that holy 'proletarian socialist revolution' which they earnestly desired to realise in 'under-developed' Japan. In their view, this ideal (but illusional) 'revolution' had to be a result of class struggle under the revolutionary leadership of the vanguard party. From this perspective, for the scholars who adhered to a dogmatic orthodox Marxism, the 1989 Eastern European change was 'a revolution which must not happen' or 'a revolution which cannot be interpreted from a class perspective'.

One of the most critical issues in the 'programme debates' among the Socialist Party, the Communist Party and Marxist scholars, as well as between both political parties in the 1950s and early 1960s, was whether a Japan's 'coming revolution' should be prescribed as 'one-stage socialist revolution' (the SP Programme in 1955) or as 'two stages from democratic to socialist revolution' (the CP Programme in 1961). But both sides expected a linear, step-by-step advance from a bourgeois revolution to a proletarian one, from a democratic revolution to a socialist one, from a socialist revolution to a dictatorship of the proletariat, from a working class state to a stateless communist society. They could not imagine that revolution could once more take place within socialist countries where the stage of socialist revolution had already successfully passed and the working class had seized state power.

Of course, concepts such as Antonio Gramsci's 'revolution against *Das Kapital*' as he characterised the Russian October Revolution, or 'the second supplementary revolution against Soviet bureaucracy in the distorted workers'

state' put forward by Leon Trotsky, had been introduced to
Japan in the post-war period. Under the overwhelming
influences of soviet-style Marxism–Leninism in Japan,
however, Gramscian Marxism or Western-style neo-Marx-
ism (or post-Marxism) which succeeded Gramscian thought
remained a minority view in Japanese Marxism. Trotsky was
labelled 'the enemy of Leninism' at the time of the
Comintern, and could not be rehabilitated in Japan.
Further, non-Marxist academic studies on revolution in
American and European sociological or political science
such as those of Barrington Moore Jr, Samuel Huntington,
Charles Tilly, Peter Calvert or Theda Skocpol, were long
ignored by reason of their lack of clear socialist sympathy to
the Russian or Chinese Revolution.

## THE 'CIVIL REVOLUTION' SCHOOL AND ITS REACTION

I myself described the 1989 Eastern European changes as a
chain of revolutions, because they had such qualities as, first,
the rapid condensed transformation of political power
relations, and secondly, the qualitative changes of the
principle of general social arrangements 'from monolithism
to pluralism' in the realms of politics, economy, culture and
ideology.

I identified the content of these events as 'democratic
revolutions', and I called them 'civil revolutions' due to the
role of non-class agents, 'a chain of peaceful revolutions in
the age of TV and rapid information spread' due to their
form, and 'revolutions through civic forums and round
tables' in their organisation.

Some other intellectuals also treated the Eastern European
transformation as a 'civil revolution'. A popular progressive
magazine, *Sekai* (World) (*Iwanami-shoten*) entitled its April
1990 special issue, *The Eastern European Revolution and
Socialism :what Happened?* This was mainly a collection of
contemporary Western arguments, including a *Die Zeit*
symposium and comments on the events by Japanese
intellectuals. The editors who arranged and commented on
this special issue were two Japanese non-Marxist political
scientists, Shimotomai Nobuo and Takahashi Susumu, who
belong to the post-war generation and have no particular
connection with the 1950s programme debates in Marxist
circles.

They wrote 'All the Eastern European societies have

achieved complete "civil" revolution for the first time 200 years after the French Revolution.' Further, 'There is no other case in modern history that such a great political change was brought about by such orderly mass movements of the citizens, and was mainly achieved without blood except in Romania . . . It was the political and social maturity of citizens that made it possible to blame the over-rigid system and to overthrow it.' *Sekai* also arranged a special issue of 'Post-revolutionary Europe' (October 1990), and argued the positive sides of the '1989 Revolution'.

At this point, I should explain to non-Japanese readers that the French phrase *révolution bourgeoise* was originally translated into Japanese in two ways. One was *burujoa kakumei* (bourgeois revolution), and the other, *shimin kakumei* (civil revolution). The former translation (*burujoa kakumei*) accented the transformation of the relations of production or ownership which opened the door to political domination of the bourgeoisie and capitalist development. The latter (*shimin kakumei*, civil revolution) focused on the mass agents of the revolution who were emancipated from the hierarchic order of the feudal social status.

When I and some other Japanese scholars named the Eastern European changes 'civil revolutions', we implied that these countries witnessed the 'formation of civil society' according to the latter meaning of the Japanese translation of *révolution bourgeoise*. It has a slightly different nuance for example from Professor Rejoi's usage of 'civil revolution' in Western social sciences (Mostafa Rejoi with Kay Phillips, *Leaders of Revolution*, Sage, 1979, p. 83).

From a standpoint similar to our interpretation of 'civil revolution', Kurihara Akira, another political scientist, paid attention to 'the eager demand for confirmation of their identity when East German people cried '*Wir sind das Volk*' in the 1989 East German Revolution', and to the 'organisational form of the civic forum, which was not a tree-type political party but a rhizome-type network' (his article in the special issue of *Asahi Journal Weekly*, 20 June 1990).

However, a book entitled *The Eastern European Reform (Tōuōu Kaikaku)* edited by Minamizuka Shingo and Miyajima Naoki published in March 1990 (Kōdansha), the same month my book *The East European Revolution and Socialism* and the special issue of *Sekai* were published, took a different view. The book was a collection of articles on the political process of each Eastern European country:

'Reform in Hungary', 'Reform in Poland', 'Reform in Bulgaria', etc. But there was only one chapter which had the title of 'revolution': ' "Revolution" in Romania'.

Neither the author of that chapter, nor the editors of the book, explained why they called the Romanian case a 'revolution', and all the others 'reform'. But we might suppose that they found the Romanian case to be a 'revolution' by virtue of its bloody process, as in the case of the *Asahi-shinbun*.

Further possible interpretation as to why the authors of this book did not call the other cases 'revolution' but 'reform', might be their academic background as Japanese historians. In Japanese historical studies, very different from those in political science, a strong influence of orthodox Marxism, characterised by economic determinism and class reductionism, remains dominant (cf. Taguchi Fukuji and Katô Tetsuro, 'Marxists' Debates on the State in Post-war Japan', *Hôsei Ronshû, Nagoya University, No. 105, August 1985*).

At the 1990 annual conference of the Historical Science Society of Japan in May, a session was held on 'Democracy in Contemporary Socialism'. All three presentations there treated the events in 1989 Eastern Europe, but none characterised them as a 'revolution'. Some famous historians personally commented to me that my work was useful, except for my questionable characterisation of the events as a 'civil revolution'.

In a monthly journal of the Historical Society of Japan, an article even appeared that claimed 'the year 1989 in East Germany was neither revolution nor democratisation, but it was caused by romanticist enthusiasm for national unity' (Hoshino Haruhiko, 'The Fall of "Revolution" and the Future of United Germany', *Rekishigaku-Kenkyû*, October 1990).

According to the traditional Marxist view of 'revolution' the 1989 Eastern European Revolution seemed to represent a reverse course against so-called historical materialism. The dominant view should rather call it a 'counter-revolution', because 'the state power of the working class' was dramatically overthrown by the people, and the historical degeneration of economic social formations began 'from socialism to capitalism', a reverse course against the hypothesis of historical materialism. But no one frankly expressed the feeling that they had witnessed 'counter-revolutions in Eastern Europe'. Some Marxists might whisper this at informal meetings, but no one published.

In such an atmosphere, it was probably intellectually honest that Professor Hiromatsu Wataru, a well-known anti-Stalinist, Marxist philosopher of the University of Tokyo, bravely proclaimed 'the bankruptcy of the Stalinist system, a bureaucratic state socialism, which was essentially unreasonable under the imperialist surrounding', and claimed that 'the day of a new, genuine Marxist world revolution will surely come' (*Shisō*, February 1990).

IMPACTS ON PARTY POLITICS – FROM THE 'SP-CGP-DSP' BLOC TO THE 'LDP-CGP-DSP'

At the level of party politics in Japan, the political parties reacted sensitively and quickly to the Eastern European Revolution because there was the 39th Lower House (General) election in February 1990.

The Eastern European change did not become the main issue in the campaign, but it indirectly affected the results of the election: the victory of the Socialist Party (SP) from 85 seats in the previous election to 136, the decrease but unexpected maintenance of a stable majority by the Liberal Democratic Party (LDP) from 300 to 275, and the defeat of small parties, that is, the Kōmeitō Party (Clean Government Party = CGP) from 56 to 45, the Japanese Communist Party (JCP) from 27 to 16, and the Democratic Socialist Party (DSP) from 26 to 14.

The governing LDP, of course, proclaimed as part of its campaign 'the collapse of socialism and communism' and 'the triumph of free society', aiming to reverse its disadvantageous position caused by the Recruit Company's financial scandal, the introduction of a general sales tax, and the defeat in the 1989 summer Upper House election.

The presidential address by the Prime Minister Kaifu Toshiki at the 52nd party convention of the LDP on 20 January 1990, just before the Lower House election, proclaimed 'The fearful politics of communism and the inefficient socialist-controlled economy were dramatically destroyed. Peoples in Eastern Europe set new goals of freedom, democracy and a market economy. "Socialism" is removed even from the names of these countries . . . The new currents in today's world proved to us that our choice of values and system such as freedom, democracy and the market economy was surely right' (*Jiyū Minshū* [LDP Monthly], March 1990).

Although the proclamation of 'the triumph of free society' did not become the critical issue of the election, the LDP gained an unexpected majority which enabled it to continue its stable domination. In a summer seminar of the LDP, Mr Kaifu introduced an episode from his visit to Poland in which Lech Walesa, the chair of *Solidarnosc*, said directly to him 'We would like to become the second Japan,' and Kaifu relaxed his position on giving economic aid to yesterday's main enemy, the former Soviet Union (*Jiyū Minshū*, September 1990).

The Democratic Socialist Party (DSP) was a right-wing social democratic party, founded by the separation from the SP in 1960, and a member of the Socialist International. The year 1990 was thus the 30th anniversary of its founding. After the party's defeat in the General Election, the 35th party convention in April 1990 welcomed 'the collapse of communism' against which the DSP had struggled for a long time. But the DSP itself had 'democratic socialism' as the final goal in its party programme. In the convention, people raised the arguments that words like 'democratic socialism' or 'socialisation of industry' should be cut from the programme, and even that the party itself had to be renamed.

These arguments related to a policy choice, whether the DSP should continue to work toward an opposition government with the SP and the CGP against the LDP (*Shakōmin*-bloc) or whether it should change its line toward building a coalition government with the LDP and the CGP (*Jikōmin*-bloc). The convention chose Ouchi Keigo as the new chairman, and he insisted on moving toward a coalition with the LDP and CGP (*Jikōmin*-bloc). Under his leadership, the DSP proceeded to bid 'farewell to socialism' and to work for a coalition with the LDP. The 36th party convention in February 1991 proposed a draft of a new party programme that substituted 'liberty, equity, fraternity and international cooperation' for 'democratic socialism'.

In its party programme (1964), the Kōmeitō (CGP) had also as a final goal the achievement of the 'humanity socialism' as well as 'buddhist democracy'. After the shock of the election defeat, it also began to re-examine its party programme. The 28th party convention in April 1990 shifted political line more clearly from 'socialist' to 'centrist'. At the

29th convention in November 1990,the party admitted the future possibility of a coalition government with the LDP.

The 1989 Eastern European Revolution forced the Japanese centrist parties, namely the DSP and the CGP, to erase the 'socialist' colours from their party programmes, and changed their orientation from an opposition bloc allied with the SP to a governmental bloc allied with the LDP. This change of course worked to the relative advantage of the LDP, which had already lost the majority in the Upper House voting. In fact, the LDP barely managed to pass a bill for 9 billion dollars in financial aid to the Coalition Force for the Gulf War in 1991, and did so only with the support of the DSP and the CGP in the Diet.

The breakdown of the 'too hard dictatorship' of the Communist Party in the single party system under state socialism in Eastern Europe has ironically brought the survival of a 'softer single party dictatorship' of the Liberal Democratic Party within the multi-party and free election system under advanced capitalism in Japan.

## THE TRANSFORMATION OF THE SPJ TO
## A SOCIAL DEMOCRATIC PARTY

The Socialist Party of Japan (*Nihon-shakaitō*, SP) is also a member of the Socialist International, but it included many non-communist Marxists. In contrast with Europe, where communist parties were once founded by separating from socialist parties in the late 1910s and early 1920s, and once more reverted to social democratic parties as a result of the Eastern European Revolution, pre-war socialist parties in Japan started only after the foundation of the Communist Party (1922), and they were mainly led by the members who once belonged to the Communist Party and later left it. The post-war foundation of the Socialist Party of Japan was also based on Marxist strategy, and the party sometimes competed with the CP in maintaining close connections with the former Soviet Union, China and North Korea.

The founding resolution of SP (1955) vowed to destroy capitalism, to put socialism in practice, and to stabilise and raise the people's living standards. The formal party programme (1955) prescribed 'a socialist revolution through democratic and peaceful ways to overcoming communism'. 'The Road towards Socialism in Japan' a programme-like resolution in 1964, criticised 'the tendency of revisionist capitalism and reformism within the Socialist International' to which the SP itself belonged as a member.

In reality, however, the SP strongly depended on the left-wing trade unions, the General Council of Trade Unions in Japan (Sōhyō), and ideologically consisted of an amalgam of Marxists, trade unionists, union bureaucrats and local activists.

Thus, leftist groups within the party held strong antipathy toward social democracy. The party statute sought not only 'to realise socialist revolution', but it also called for 'democratic centralism' in party discipline, just the same as the CP organisation, although there were in fact continual factional struggles for the leading posts or policy lines. Some Marxist party members even called their own party *Shamin*, jargon Japanese for 'social democracy'. In fact, the formal English party name of *Nihon-shakaitō* had previously been translated as 'the Social Democratic Party of Japan' from 1955 to 1964. But it was changed to 'the Socialist Party of Japan' in 1964, when 'the Road toward Socialism in Japan' was adopted.

Considering all these points, the fall of Eastern European socialism and *perestroika* in the Soviet Union should have damaged the SP. However, the SP had already partly begun to break from soviet-type socialism and to transform itself to a Western-type social democratic party in the early 1980s, and it made an effort to build an opposition bloc with the CGP, without the CP. It also adopted a resolution for 'Creation of a New Society – A Design of our Socialism' (1982) which clearly denied the soviet-type socialism.

The 1986 platform of 'The New Manifesto of the SP – Creation by the power of love and knowledge' was the turning point from a revolutionary socialist party to a reformist social democratic party, although even this platform did not use the word 'social democracy', due to the resistance of leftist opposition groups within the party. Japanese media called this change 'The Birth of a New SP'.

It should be noted, however, that this new course of the SP in 1986 did not mean that the SP had become close to the new Western social democratic programmes such as the Stockholm Manifesto of the Socialist International or the Berlin Programme of the German Social Democratic Party (SPD), both of which were adopted in 1989 and absorbed such new social values as ecology, feminism and the re-examination of economic growth, influenced by new social movements. Rather, the 1986 'New Manifesto of the SP' was a 30-years-late catch-up to the level of the 1951 Frankfurt Manifesto of the Socialist International or the 1959 Bad-Godesberg Programme of the SPD, which had declared goals of becoming a 'national governable party' and 'a welfare state with mixed economy'.

Based on this 'New Manifesto' the SP elected Ms Doi Takako as the chair in 1987, and won the 1989 Upper House election. There was a 'New SP boom' when the SP opposed the general sales tax and put forward many women candidates, supported by grassroots movements of citizens in summer 1989. This was the background that allowed the SP to escape from the negative 'collapse of socialism' campaign of the LDP and make gains in the 1990 General Election. The 1989 Eastern European Revolution forced the complete transformation of the SP from a revolutionary socialist party to a reformist social democratic party. The 55th party convention in April 1990 was the occasion for this reconstruction. The resolution analysed the Eastern European Revolution as follows:

'The energy for reform by the citizens in Eastern Europe led to the Post-Cold War era, ended the long single-party dictatorship by communist parties, and is transforming Eastern Europe to social democracy which posits liberty, equity, cohabitation, solidarity, human rights and democracy as basic values.' Also, 'social democracy today forms a large belt-zone in the whole of Europe and is becoming the leading power of international society in the coming 21st century' (*Gekkan Shakaitō* [SP Monthly], June 1990).

Ms Doi Takako, the chairperson, called for the 'creation of a Japanese road of social democracy' at the convention. Such words as 'socialist revolution' or 'democratic centralism' were cut from the new party statutes. The formal English translation of the party's name went back to 'the Social Democratic Party of Japan'. But this reformist transformation on the surface does not mean a change in the weak party structure in which a mere 128,000 party members are able to win 17 million votes and over 200 seats in the Diet.

It seems uncertain whether the SP can keep up the so-called 'New SP boom'. In fact, the victory of the SPJ in the 1989/1990 national elections was made possible only by the scandalous errors of the LDP. This victory postponed the more serious policy choice needed by the SP to become a governable party in the face of the great transformation of the world order.

## THE FALL OF THE COMINTERN'S TRADITION AND THE ISOLATION OF THE JCP

The Eastern European Revolution of course exerted the most negative impact on the Japanese Communist Party, because it was founded in 1922 as the Japanese section of the Communist International (Comintern, 1919–1943) as were the Eastern European communist parties overthrown by the 1989 Revolution. The JCP had already been defeated in the 1989 summer Upper House election, influenced by the Chinese Tiananmen Square Incident and it once more lost in the 1990 Lower House election. In fact, the JCP had debated with the Soviet and Chinese communist parties for 30 years, seeking 'self-independence' within the international communist movement against Soviet or Chinese hegemonic attitudes and interference in other communist parties. But it was natural for Japanese voters that people overlapped the images of Chinese, Soviet or Eastern European communists with the JCP, because they were all named 'communists' as the indispensable condition for the historical foundation of the parties within the Comintern.

The overlap of the image of the JCP with the reality of communist dictatorship in other countries also derived from the JCP's rigid propaganda that it was always right because its theory of 'scientific socialism' was an *a priori* 'truth' and that others were always wrong, from its closed monolithic' secret-style organisation caused by the 'democratic centralist' tradition of the Comintern, or from the more than 30 years of personal leadership by Miyamoto Kenji, the 81-year-old chairman.

The JCP had a long history of recognising the Soviet Union or Eastern Europe as 'the socialist states', or 'communist comrade parties', even though after the 1970s the JCP added the reservation that they were not 'an ideal socialism' but 'socialism in a growing process'. The JCP had especially close connections with the Romanian Ceausescu government because both parties had a common inter-communist diplomatic policy of 'self-independence' against the CPSU. The Ceausescu–Miyamoto statements in 1971, 1978 and 1987 were recent important achievements of the JCP's international activity.

Of course, the JCP did not conceive the Eastern European changes as 'revolutions'. According to the definition of *The Dictionary of Social Science* which the JCP mainly edited (second edition, Shinnihon-shuppansha, Tokyo, February 1989), 'revolution' means, 'substitution of an old economic social formation for a new one (social revolution), especially, a transformation of agents of state power from one class or some classes to another class or classes (political revolution)'. If the 1989 Eastern European changes could be recognised as a 'revolution', it would suggest a bankruptcy of the theoretical consistency of so-called 'scientific socialism' for the JCP.

The resolution of the 19th party congress of the JCP (July 1990) explained that 'the Eastern European upheaval *(gekiben)* revealed the bankruptcy of the Stalin-Brezhnev-type political-economic system and its great power coercion of Eastern Europe . . . It did not mean the breakdown of socialism itself but the failure of governments or parties which were misnamed socialist until today.'

The JCP was proud that it had criticised the political lines of the Soviet Union, China and Eastern European communists long before they were destroyed, relying upon 'the principle of scientific socialism and self-independence,' and that it had affirmed free elections with a multi-party system as the basic policy for Japanese socialism since 1976, when it adopted 'The Manifesto for Freedom and Democracy' at the 13th party congress. For the JCP, the 1917 Russian socialist revolution and the policies thereafter under the leadership by Lenin were undoubtedly 'right' and valuable. The 'failure' began only after Stalin distorted the Leninist lines, and Brezhnev continued this 'failure' *(Zenei* [JCP Monthly], September 1990).

These interpretations, of course, could not enable many intellectuals to understand the situation. I and another 14 intellectuals, including supporters of the JCP who expected its role to check LDP-domination or to democratise Japan's business-orientated society, contributed to a book, *Letters to the JCP* (Kyoiku-Shiryo-Shuppankai, Tokyo, June 1990), and proposed some survival policies and advice for the JCP. But the JCP leaders not only denied our proposals concerning the 'civil revolution' line or the 'democratisation of party organisation' by learning from the Eastern European lessons, but also attacked us for our 'anti-communist propaganda'.

This showed how extremely different the position of

today's JCP is from the Italian Communist Party which obviously had the similar policies of 'Euro-Japan-Communism'. For the JCP, the renaming of the ICP as the Italian Left Democratic Party was 'a corruption into social democracy'. Even Gorbachev's 'New Thinking' in his world policy was rejected by the JCP, by reason of his priority on human beings and ecological issues over the class struggles. As for party organisation, the JCP maintained the traditional line of 'democratic centralism'. Miyamoto Kenji, was re-elected as the chair. Members disobedient to the central committee were denounced as 'opportunists', and their voices were not heard at the party congress.

But even within the JCP, the 1989 Eastern European Revolution surely made an impact. There were many critical opinions voiced against the JCP leaders and their policies at the discussions of the draft of resolution before the 19th congress. One observer commented that the inner-party opposition to the draft resolution during the discussion on the organ reached about one-third of the total. After the congress, some JCP members who were in local assemblies left the party.

The JCP seems to have run into a dead-end, losing a chance to transform itself that will not recur.

## CRISIS? POSSIBILITY FOR REBIRTH? OR THE END OF SOCIALISM? – ARGUMENTS AMONG LEFT INTELLECTUALS

The strong influence of Marxism in Japanese universities and academic circles is well known. For example, many national universities traditionally have two educational courses in economic theory. One is Marxist, and the other is modern neo-classical or Keynesian economics. In such circumstances, there were also various arguments on the Eastern European changes among Marxist intellectuals.

As I have already noted, many scholars who believed in the orthodox soviet-type Marxism and placed hopes for the future in 'actually existing socialism', could not understanding the situation. They mainly kept silent. Intellectuals who supported the SP or the JCP avoided interpreting it as a 'revolution', and mentioned it only as 'reform' or 'democratisation'. Almost all Japanese Marxists experienced ambivalent feelings, akin to those of East German intellectuals, who were once the driving force of a revolution for 'democratic socialism', but who became a minority soon

146

after the fall of the Berlin Wall under the pressure of the people's desire for national unity of *Wir sind ein Volk*.

Opinions of seven Marxist economists who were interviewed in the February 1990 issue of *Bungei Shunju* represented this ambivalence. The question was, 'Has Marxism died?' The seven answers differed in nuance, but the following views were held in common:

(1) The soviet-type or Stalinist socialism under one-party dictatorship and centralist economic system had collapsed.

(2) But this had never been the realisation of Karl Marx's original image of socialism, because Russia before the 1917 resolution was not an advanced capitalist country.

(3) This soviet-type socialism was not typical socialism in Marx's sense. Thus, its breakdown did not mean the collapse of 'socialism in general'.

(4) Marxism did not confront its death, but a crisis. This crisis was also a necessary precondition of its rebirth.

(5) For this rebirth, Japanese Marxists should take more seriously, on the one hand, the post-war European experiences of social democratic welfare states like West Germany or Sweden.

(6) On the other hand, advanced capitalism also faces many unresolvable problems. Therefore, the East European changes meant neither the death of Marxism nor the triumph of capitalism.

There were, of course, some sincere scholars who seriously recognised that a revolutionary transformation had taken place against socialism, and they made efforts to understand it through their own self-criticism. Kamijima Takeshi, an economist for example, analysed it as a 'revolution with neither revolutionary theory nor revolutionary party', and characterised is as 'not a workers' revolution, but a civil revolution' (*Mado*, No. 4, summer 1990).

In his article entitled 'Epistemology of the Eastern European Civil Revolution', Hirata Kiyoaki, a well-known economist, described it as 'a social political change promoted by electronification and globalisation with the same causes as that of the completing of the enlarged EC market'. He also noted, 'The party-state system which named itself "socialism" was defeated by the dynamism of capitalism, characterised not only by its parasitism but also by its creative destruction' (*Keizai Kyōron*, October 1990).

The February 1991 special issue of *Jōkyō*, a Japanese-style new-left journal carried such articles as that of Hisashi Nagao, who argued that 'the 1989 National-Democratic Revolution in Eastern Europe saw the revival of national history in each country', and Ishizuka Shoji who stressed the character of a 'revolution toward capitalism brought by intellectuals'.

About the historical meaning of these events for socialism, I and some others argued for considering them 'the general crisis of socialism' (Katō in *The Eastern European Revolution and Socialism*, Iwata Masayuki in *Keizai-Seminar*, October 1989, Yoshiaki Nishimura in *Mado*, No. 2, winter 1989). In contrast to the title of my book *The Crisis of Socialism and the Rebirth of Democracy* (July 1990), a book by Iida Momo, a famous new-left leader, was entitled *The End of Socialism and the Catastrophe of Capitalism* (Shakai-hyoronsha, Tokyo, December 1990).

The arguments at the founding conference of the 'Forum '90s' in December 1990 encapsulated the perception of the Eastern European Revolution by Japanese left-wing intellectuals. This 'Forum '90s' was a networking organisation of about 800 left intellectuals and activists. It was a new attempt to overcome the deeply rooted political or sectarian conflicts endemic in Japanese left-wing groups.

The most controversial argument involved, (1) the 'civil revolution' group which found positive sides in the democratic socialist ideal in 1989 Eastern Europe (I and Hirata Kiyoaki), (2) 'the fall of socialism' group which stressed the critical side of the 'ethical defeat of socialism' (Horikawa Satoshi), the 'historical downfall of Marxism' (Doi Shukuhei), or the 'revolution toward capitalism' (Ishizuka Shoji), (3) the 'toward a genuine socialist revolution' group who still believed in 'a coming mass-revolt-type revolution at the third stage of Marxism' (Hiromatsu Wataru), and also (4) the 'new social movement' groups in Japanese style like ecology, feminism, peace and anti-nuclear movements, cooperative networking and local grassroots movements.

But all these groups required in common 'a new framework of knowledge for subject emancipation' (the appeal at the foundation of 'Forum '90s'), for they recognised the crisis not only of the social orientation but also of grassroots democracy in Japanese capitalism. The common goal was 'to solve subjectively the crisis we face, and to design a new society without exploitation, for the survival of human beings and the maintenance of the earth, through solidarity with multiple movements growing in Japan and other regions of the world' (founding manifesto).

The foundation of 'Forum '90s' implied an experiment of intellectual networking by the Japanese left, learning from the Eastern European Revolution 'through civic forums and round tables'.

## 'THE TRIUMPH OF CAPITALISM?' – LESSONS FOR JAPANESE BUSINESS LEADERS

In more popular perceptions of the Eastern European events in Japan, mass media and mass magazines played a critical role.

The *Asahi-shinbun* interviewed 15 Japanese politicians, scholars and business leaders in April and May 1990, asking 'Where does socialism go?' The issues below were not very different from the European or American discussion: (1) the lack of democracy under the dictatorship by communist parties in actually existing socialism, (2) the failure of the planned economy using nationalisation and central control without the market, (3) the delay of technical innovation which prevented adaptation to the soft and service-orientated economy of an information society, (4) the theoretical origin of the failure of socialism in Stalin, Lenin or Marx, (5) the end of the historical separation between socialism (social democracy) and communism, (6) the implication of the fall of socialism for the capitalist world, (7) the role of nationalism and religion in the transformation.

*Bungei Shunju* and the *Chūō Kōron*, very popular monthly magazines among not only intellectuals but also business leaders and white collar workers, wrote in sensational fashion concerning the 'collapse of socialism' with articles as 'The World Changed! – How should the Western Bloc Treat the End of Socialism', 'A Long Path to the Breakdown of Soviet Dictatorship' and so forth. The dominant issues there were not the future of the Soviet Union, Eastern Europe or socialism, but its meaning for international relations, especially its effects on the Japanese economy, with articles like 'The Post-Malta World', 'Eastern European Aid – What is the Lesson from the Marshall Plan', 'The Cold War is not Finished', 'The Collapse of the

Communist Bloc and US–Japan Relations', 'Japanese Economy will not sink', and so forth.

However, talk of 'the collapse of socialism' or 'the triumph of capitalism' reflected only a superficial mood. There were not many arguments which praised 'the triumph of capitalism'. For example, Makino Noboru, the president of the Mitsubishi Research Institute, answered to the *Asahi-shinbun* interview, 'We should seriously analyse the events and ask whether they were essentially caused by socialism or by the wearing out of the system of one-party dictatorship.' Kawai Ryōichi, the president of the Komatsu Corporation and a vice-president of Keidanren (Federation of Economic Organisations of Japan), also responded, 'The social democratic system which introduced some elements of a capitalist market system will remain, instead of the former very rigid socialism.' These statements implied that Japanese business leaders should draw lessons from the Eastern European or Soviet experience.

What kind of lessons did Japanese business leaders draw? The article 'Capitalism will also collapse, if it remains as it is today – What Japanese should learn from the Fall of Communism' by Inamori Kazuo, the president of the Kyocera Corporation, was typical (*The Voice*, May 1990).

Inamori wrote 'The fall of communist systems in Eastern Europe should not be seen only as the triumph of liberalism or capitalism against communism, or the victory of a market economy against the breakdown of the planned economy. We need two more perspectives. One stresses the under-estimation of the spirituality of human beings. The other reconfirms the people's power'. This 'under-estimation of spirituality' meant for him that 'Man shall not live by bread alone'. He pointed out that the Soviet economy lost the holy mission which surely existed at the first stage of the October Revolution, and was harmed by flaws of economy-centralism such as the decrease of morality, the passive completion of assigned jobs, or authoritarian labour control. He also added, 'Such an atmosphere also grows in capitalism, due to the vulgar incentive for sales only, the materialistic advertisements which stimulate consumers' desire, and the mammonism which worships money only.' He in turn mentioned, 'Recent students in Japan who studied engineering at university do not choose jobs in manufacturing but in banks or securities companies. The younger generations avoid making the effort of entering the manufacturing world.' He gave a warning, 'If we proceed in this way, our capitalist world may also become bankrupt in the same way as the communist world.' His second point, 'the reconfirmation of people's power' implied that we are now in 'the age of the revival of people's power under the decreased authority of state power, where recent people's revolts showed the system can not continue if it loses legitimacy.'

In the case of Japan, there remained (1) 'the bureaucratic organisations which control very expensive air fares or taxi fees', and (2) 'the existence of giant corporations which monopolise the market and conceal information'. He found it possible that people's revolt would occur against these two authorities in the name of 'people's power' in Japan also. In addition, he warned, (3) 'Japanese people might confront worldwide people's power directed against them, if they could not contribute to the global ecological problems taking serious responsibility as an advanced country'.

Although this argument was not raised by the *zaibatsu*-type business group like Mitsui or Mitsubishi, but by the leader of a typical venture business in Japan, it showed one essential lesson of the 1989 Revolutions in Eastern Europe for the Japanese business world.

## THE MINIMUM SOCIALIST ORIENTATION IN JAPAN AND THE MAXIMUM 'LEARNING FROM JAPAN' BOOM IN THE FORMER SOVIET UNION AND EASTERN EUROPE

Indeed, the objects of Mr Inamori's concern, economy-centred feelings and materialism, dominated the popular Japanese perception of Eastern European changes. In politics, 'the one-party dictatorship with a multi-party system and free elections' continued. In culture, the dominant arguments about the Eastern European events focused not on democracy or freedom, but on economic aspects like 'the failure of the planned economy' or 'the delay in innovation and the shortage of goods in socialism'. There were numerous reasons why such feelings dominated.

The popular consciousness of 'the defeat of socialism and communism' or 'the triumph of liberalism and capitalism' had already been established during the rapid economic growth of the 1960s and 1970s.

A general public opinion poll, *A Study of Japanese National Character*, by the Institute of Statistical Mathematics (ISM) provides us interesting data relevant to the immediate question of 'What do you think about socialism?' The answer 'socialism is good' (the other two choices were 'depends on circumstances' and 'bad') declined from 34 per cent in 1958 to 15 per cent in 1963, then to 14 per cent in 1973. Regrettably, there is no data on this question thereafter. But my own research asking the same question to students of political science at Hitotsubashi University showed a continual decline in the responses 'socialism is good', even among students who were thought relatively more radical than the average. The students who answered 'socialism is good' at Hitotsubashi University numbered 11 per cent in 1985, and this decreased to only 4 per cent in April 1989, just before the Tiananmen Square incidents in China.

In contrast with 'socialism is good', the answer 'capitalism is good' in the ISM poll was given by only 12 per cent in 1958 (under half the number who said 'socialism is good'). This increased to 19 per cent in 1963 (surpassing 'socialism is good') but slightly decreased to 17 per cent in 1973 due to the high inflation and the price rise just before the first oil crisis. The ratio of students responding 'capitalism is good' was already 20 per cent in 1985, and this reached 30 per cent in 1989. The answers 'liberalism is good' and 'democracy is good' were of course always much more numerous than 'capitalism is good', and the veto answer of 'communism is bad' was always much more common than 'socialism is bad' (*A Study of Japanese National Character*, Part 3, Idemitsu-shoten, Tokyo, 1975).

Another poll on 'Consciousness of Working' in which freshly-recruited workers have been asked by the Japan Productivity Centre about their attitude to work each year since 1970 shows this historical tendency much more clearly. The question was 'What kind of society do you wish, while Japanese society is called a capitalist society?' The answer had to be chosen from among 'preservation of today's system', and 'no concern'. The graphic figure of the answers for these 20 years from 1970 through 1990 (see next page) shows that the socialist orientation of new workers stood at 10 per cent at the time of the first oil crisis, but decreased to 2 per cent even before the 1989 revolutions and fell to the extreme minority of 1 per cent after the revolutions by reason of the spread of conservatism among the younger generation.

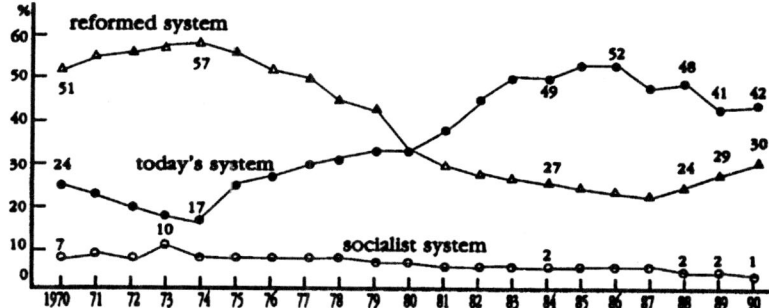

An interesting result of this research emerges by comparing these answers about social systems with data on party support. The data in 1990 showed that the SP was supported by 10.5 per cent of the whole. Yet over 40 per cent of SP supporters called for 'preservation of today's system' and only 3.6 per cent chose 'socialism'. The JCP was chosen in only 1.2 per cent of all the answers. Twenty per cent of these wished for 'preservation of today's system'. I call this historical decline of the socialist orientation in Japanese popular consciousness 'the birth of the socialist ghetto society'.

One more important point here is the attitude toward Japan of the people in the former Soviet Union or Eastern European countries. When Lech Walesa, the chair of Solidarity at the time and now the President of Poland, confessed his dream that Poland might become 'the second Japan', it stimulated the pride of Japanese. Many Soviet and Eastern European leaders in economics and politics recently visited Japan to learn the so-called 'Japanese model' or 'Japanese management'. They admired the success story of the Japanese economy so enthusiastically that this hot air caused an infection of Japanese nationalist feelings.

Some visitors from former socialist countries even found evidence of 'a genuine socialist achievement in Japan'. They noted such elements as proof for 'socialism in Japan' as the relative equality in income distribution, the success of long-term economic planning through the famous (or notorious in Western countries!) administrative guidance of the market economy of the Ministry of International Trade and Industry

153

(MITI) without nationalisation of the means of production, the high productivity and the high quality goods based on the cooperation between labour and capital, or Japanese-style collectivism. If these provide evidence of 'a genuine socialism', perhaps I would add 'the soft and flexible single-party dictatorship of the LDP through free elections with a multi-party system' as further proof!

Although such extreme admiration (or insult?) was exceptional, visitors from former socialist countries tended to look for only the productive and bright sides of Japanese society, without looking at the seamy sides. They passionately desired to learn from Japanese experiences, because they found a superior model for their problems of economic reconstruction in Japanese history. For example, the Japanese lessons from the sell-off of national industries in the Meiji period, the rapid economic recovery controlled by the strong central government after the defeat of the Second World War, the privatisation of the National Railways or the Telegraphy & Telephone Public Corporation by the Nakasone government in the 1980s, all meant Japan offered a more realistic and more introductory case study for their learning about the capitalist economy than those in Western Europe or the USA, where there was a too open free market system. For advice, they looked not to left-wing scholars who had long-standing connections with these countries, but to high governmental officials, practical business leaders, or non-Marxist, right-wing economists (cf. *Anatoly Ill-arionovich Milykov's Report on Japanese Economy*, Moscow, 1991). In fact, Katō Hiroshi, a well-known LDP intellectual at Keiō University, became one of the most important advisers for the so-called 'Shatalin Plan' in the Soviet Union.

## 'A BIG BUSINESS OPPORTUNITY FOR JAPANESE'
– ECONOMY-CENTRED PERCEPTION

It was inevitable in these circumstances that there would appear such a confident perspective on the future of Japanese economy as that in the New Year address below by Tabuchi Yoshihisa, the president of the Nomura Securities Company. It symbolised the greedy entrepreneurial spirit of capital accumulation of Japanese transnational corporations that grasped even the Eastern European Democratic Revolution as a 'big business opportunity':

154

'The basic background of the great transformation of the world is the change from cannon to butter, namely, from ideology to economy, which is now the driving force of the world order. We are now facing tremendous business opportunities all over the world!' (*Asahi-shinbun*, 4 January 1990)

In fact, conditions in Japan did enable the Japanese people to regard such an economy-centred and arrogant statement as natural in 1989–90. The Japanese economy recorded its best performances at the time. The most popular TV commercial song in 1989 had such a text as 'Can you fight 24 hours a day for your business? Can you fight all over the world as a Japanese businessman?'

A public opinion poll by the *Asahi-shinbun* together with the US Harris Company in December 1989 showed a very characteristically divergent perception of the 1989 Revolution by Japanese and Americans. The question to Japanese and American citizens was, 'What do you think is the most fundamental desire of Eastern European people?' The answers are summarised in the table (*Asahi-shinbun*, 27 December 1989):

|  | US (average) | US (18-24 yrs old) | JAPAN (average) | JAPAN (20-24 yrs old) |
|---|---|---|---|---|
| Political Liberty to make their Own Government | 48% | 58% | 40% | 38% |
| Improvement of their Living Standards | 30% | 25% | 41% | 53% |
| Abandonment of the Failure by Communism | 17% | 17% | 8% | 7% |
| Others, NA | 5% | — | 11% | — |

In contrast to the majority of Americans who saw a desire for 'political liberty' in Eastern Europe, nearly half of the Japanese believed the Eastern Europeans were struggling for 'better living standards'. Especially interesting for me were the answers of the younger generation. The American youth sympathised with the Eastern European people from the standpoint of their own political belief in American values. The Japanese youth thought, in contrast, that the Eastern European events were caused by the economic reason of a desire for Western goods, which Japanese could easily gain and enjoy in their so-called 'affluent society'. This clearly showed, in my view, the presence of what Mr Inamori worried about in his article as economy-centralism of mammonism. It suggested that Japanese people had surely lost the spirit of 'Man shall not live by bread alone'.

## 'A FIRE ACROSS THE SEA' – PASSIVE AND DREAMLESS PERCEPTION

This economy-centred reaction to global events by the Japanese has continued to appear as they faced the end of the Cold War, German unification and the formation of new European order, and the recent Gulf Crisis and War. Japanese foreign investment has become the highest in the world, but Japanese diplomatic and military policies still strongly depend on the USA. The relatively smaller scale of Japanese investment in the former Soviet Union or Eastern Europe, compared to US or Western European capitalism, implies that Japanese capital is anxious about the economic cost, doubting the stability of Eastern European economies or Gorbachev's leadership. If the introduction of a market economy and foreign capital in the Soviet Union or Eastern Europe runs smoothly, a great amount of Japanese money will flow there. This also reveals a passive and economy-centred attitude.

The 'workaholics in rabbit hutches' situation of Japanese workers seems to continue. They work over 2,100 hours a year, about 500 hours (4 months!) more than French or Germans on average, which even results in so-called Japanese *karōshi*, the notorious 'death by overworking' (see National Defence Council for Victims of Karōshi, [Karōshi] [English Version], Mado-sha,Tokyo, 1990). Even trade unions are also proud of 'the performance of Japanese economy', although the ordinary worker cannot buy his own house with his life salary, if he lives in Tokyo. More than 10 million 'rich Japanese' visited foreign countries in 1990 for business or for sightseeing. Many Japanese travelled to Germany and toured the former Berlin Wall. But they were more enthusiastic to buy a piece of the wall as a gift rather than to communicate with German people.

These common patterns of thinking and acting among the government, corporations and the ordinary people, I believe, must confront many obstacles at the new stage of world history which began with the 1989 Eastern European Revolution. Japanese people, however, had not sufficiently discussed the meaning of the worldwide transformation before they faced the Gulf Crisis soon after the revolutions, and were forced by US pressure to pay $9 billion (¥10,000 per Japanese!) for the Coalition Force. We can find here, too, the passive and non-subjective Japanese perception of global events as 'a fire across the sea'.

The dominant mentality in Japan's 'affluent society', one which has supported the success of Japanese management, is this passive and selfish concern for their daily life, which I call 'conservatism in private life.' But one may raise the question whether such conservatism was not maintained also by the Eastern European people for a long time, until 1989, under the communist regimes. In Eastern Europe, the people's mentality changed rapidly from passive to active, from superficial agreement to great discontent. What Eastern European people perceived as common sense in 1988 was turned upside down in 1989. What Eastern European people felt as a 'permanent dream' until the spring of 1989 became reality in 1990.

I believe that the most important lesson from Eastern Europe for Japanese people must be to realise that 'History can be moved by the people's dreams and power'. In the early post-war period, Japanese people had their own dreams. The dreams were for 'permanent peace', 'democracy and human rights', 'catching up with Western industrial society', or 'the American way of life'. These dreams urged Japanese to work hard and to innovate in technology, and they surely became the driving force for rapid economic growth. An 'affluent society' in the materialistic sense appeared. The GNP per capita exceeded $24,000, more than that of the US or Sweden. Japan's ODA also became the highest in the world.

While the dream in economic terms was almost completely realised, the dream of political idealism was lost. After economic growth was achieved, the dreams should have shifted to the political dreams of 'permanent peace' or 'democracy', instead of 'catching up with Western industry' or 'the American way of life'. However, these could not be realised as dreamed soon after the war. This led to the curious coexistence of the Japanese Peace Constitution with the US–Japan Security Treaty and the Self-Defence Force, or of the free elections, female suffrage, and a multi-party system with over 30 years of one-party rule by the LDP.

In post-war Japan, political democratisation remained minimal, but the economic desire grew up to the maximum.

This 'maximum capitalism with minimum democracy', or 'condensed capitalism', has now created a 'dreamless society'. Neither politicians nor bureaucrats clearly display a national vision. Ordinary people have lost the feeling of historical dynamism. This 'dreamless society' causes the strange juxtaposition of 'third class politics with a first class economy' within the world system, the decline of internal vitality within Japanese corporations, or the momentary consumption boom in youth in the so-called 'new species' generation.

From the early 1950s to early 1970s, socialism was one of these beautiful dreams for the Japanese. It especially attracted the younger generation. But the success of Japanese capitalism on the one hand, and the failure of 'actually existing socialism' on the other destroyed this dreamy fascination. However, 'permanent peace', 'democratic politics', 'human rights', and 'civil society' remain alive as alternative Japanese visions. Such non-materialistic values as 'ecology', 'anti-nuclearism', 'feminism', or 'solidarity with the third world' have recently been added to the list of dreams. Will the time come when Japanese people view the 1989 Eastern European Revolutions as stimulating them to one more dream in the twenty-first century? The answer is uncertain. It should be determined by the Japanese themselves and the future of the people's power around the world.

## 11
# Yellow Athena: the Japanese model and the East European revolution

DAVID WILLIAMS

### THE ARGUMENT

THE CHIEF TASK facing the post-communist regimes of Eastern and East-Central Europe today is how to create a civil society 'from above'. No major European thinker has been more discerning about the complex interplay between the state and civil society than Hegel; no society has better demonstrated how such an interplay can be made to succeed than post-war Japan. Eastern Europeans have torn down the old Stalinist edifice, but must now attempt to create the institutions and values essential to the successful working of a civil society: this is the point where the argument must begin. The American or British free market model has been proposed as the solution to Eastern European ills. This essay asks: Might the post-war Japanese model suggest a 'third way'?

The question may be put in a still more provocative way. In a controversial 1989 essay titled 'The End of History?', Francis Fukuyama attempted to give Western capitalism's victory over communism a Hegelian gloss.[1] He argued that the end of history has eliminated all but one intellectual option for the future evolution of the planet. The 'American way of life' was canonised as the sole coherent system of values and practices; everything else was obscurant barbarism that would inevitably be scattered by the force of this new Enlightenment.

This argument, if correct, would put the political and philosophical problems of Eastern Europe in a complex and arresting light. First, the challenge of creating a civil society from above demands clarity about both the theory being applied and the practical results being pursued. This Fukuyama believes he has achieved by updating Hegel. Fukuyama rightly insists that thought and action must not be viewed as contrary modes of human behaviour, and the 'end of history', as Hegel first used the term, would weld thought and action in a powerful, directed way. Second, Fukuyama's thesis appears to give the nod to economic forces at the expense of political choice. If the end of history has truly arrived, then the political is henceforth condemned as an ontological status inferior (politics no longer counts as a first-class piece of reality) to that of the economic, where the reference is to neo-classical economic liberalism alone. Third, Fukuyama's thesis must be seen to reject as irrelevant or obscurant all the values and memories that history has hitherto grafted on to the mind of Eastern and East Central Europe. As life there has never been governed by the principles at work in the neo-conservative interpretation of the American way of life, most of the heritage of Eastern European culture is either irrelevant to its future needs or a hindrance to be discarded.

Japan's modern experience rejects all of these assumptions except the first. The Japanese model offers a subtle and complex design for fostering a civil society but one that is capable of clear statement. The Japanese example demonstrates the importance of politics as a means to achieve economic ends, yet it is no calm surrender to the arbitrary outcomes generated by market forces. It is about making things happen: setting national goals and achieving them. Political ends are given preference over economic interests. In practical terms, the Meiji reformers built their plans around the Japanese realities inherited from the Tokugawa, just as the future of Central and Eastern Europe must be built on what history and regional values have made those Europeans.

This is not to deny the attractiveness of any vision of post-communist society, as proclaimed by the neo-liberal monetarist, that would promise a fresh institutional beginning and an 'epistemological break' (to borrow a term from Althusser) with the perceived failures of communism. In fact, however, such monetarist visionaries aim to free Eastern Europe, particularly Russia and Poland, not just from the pernicious effects of communist rule but from any aspect of the national character of these peoples or their past that conspires against remaking Russians or Poles in conformity with the doctrine of 'Economic Man'. The suggestion would be that Poland, for example, has suffered from a 'captive mind' (in Czeslaw Milosz's phrase) throughout its history, rather than just during the 1940s and 1950s. Monetarism will now bring to a close the 'dark ages' that have dominated the whole of the Polish past. More radical still, monetarists demand that Russians break with their past. Given the horrors of Russian history, this is a tempting dream, but how likely is it to be realised in practice?

This, no doubt, constitutes a bold example of economic theory spinning. But it is also an impracticable programme that goes against the grain of Eastern European social reality. In contrast, the view is taken here that Eastern Europe must begin from what it is and has been. The pre-war statist tradition, the nightmare of the Second World War, and communist industrial foundations (*jūkōgyō-ka* is the Japanese term) laid between 1945 and 1989 are the defining facts of Eastern European reality today. The task of rebuilding the nation would be far easier if the mere evocation of market forces, as monetarists conceive them, could erase a thousand years of Eastern European experience, as distinct peoples, nations, and states.

Is such a philosophy in any sense persuasive? It may yet succeed; the free market model is, after all, a formidable body of theory and experience, although it sometimes appears necessary to speak English to make it work. But if modern Japan is a model that is more consistent with Eastern European realities, and can offer a reform programme more likely to succeed in today's fiercely competitive economy, then detailed examination of the Japanese model as a guide for a capitalist Eastern Europe becomes not only desirable, but essential. If the Anglo-American neo-conservative model, which presently occupies pole position, begins to falter, then it will be time for hard questions, many of them with Japanese answers.

FOOTNOTES TO HEGEL

To raise such objections is to break with the ruling assumptions, one is tempted to say dogmas, of the Anglo-American neo-liberals, those who in America are often called 'neo-conservatives', who dominate the current debate over where Eastern Europe is to go now that its anti-communist revolution has been achieved. In contrast to the Thatcherite or Friedmanite approach, it is argued here that the contemporary crisis of the Central and East European state and society is better interpreted in the strong light of Hegel's meditations, set out in his *Philosophy of Right*.[2] The experience of post-war Japan will be used to give concrete meaning to Hegel's abstract schema.

If List may be regarded as the European godfather of the Japanese economic miracle, then perhaps Hegel may be one of Europe's most fruitful thinkers, *avant la lettre*, about the nineteenth and twentieth century experience of the Japanese state. Certainly no political philosopher working in the Anglo-American tradition has matched the insights of Germans such as Hegel into the Japanese model. This Hegelian gesture to an oriental polity has found a contemporary echo in the Continental European tradition. It may be no accident that the most famous, because most intriguing, footnote in all European writing about Japan is by an Hegelian. It occurs in *The Introduction to the Reading of Hegel*, the collection of Alexandre Kojève's celebrated lectures on Hegel's *Phenomenology of Spirit* (1807), delivered at the École des Hautes Études in Paris between 1953 and 1959. In the second edition of these lectures, the author observes:

'Now, several voyages of comparison made (between 1949 and 1958) to the United States and the USSR gave me the impression that if the Americans give the appearance of being rich Sino-Soviets, it is because the Russians and Chinese are only Americans who are still poor but are rapidly proceeding to get richer. I was able to conclude from this that the "American way of life" was the type of life specific to the post-historical period, the actual presence of the United States in the World prefiguring the "eternal present" future of all humanity. . . . It was following a recent voyage to Japan (1959) that I had a radical change of opinion on this point. There I was able to observe a Society that is one of a kind, because it alone has for almost three centuries experienced life at the "end of History". . . . This seems to allow one to believe that the recently begun interaction between Japan and the Western world will finally lead not to a rebarbarisation of the Japanese but to a "Japanisation" of the Westerners (including the Russians).'[3]

Kojève's peripatetic meditations are pregnant with insight. In the light of the Revolution of 1989–90 in East-Central Europe, the crushing of the student protest in Tiananmen Square in June 1989, and the present wave of tumultuous

162

change engulfing the Soviet Union, the question of whether Sino-Soviet Man is merely an impoverished version of American Man looms large. Is it true that only the slightest adjustment of the Chinese and Russian mentality, combined with the freeing of market forces, will transform these societies into vibrant capitalist nations? On the other hand, if Japan is the key exception to the American way of life then this, too, is an issue of some moment in the reformation of economic and social life as it is lived in Eastern and East-Central Europe.

It has been dogmatically asserted that the neo-liberal model of Hayek, Friedman and Thatcher is the only way of addressing the problems of Eastern Europe. But this model is not consistent with the region's history or with the religious and ideological evolution of these European peoples or with their varied national characters. It is being insisted upon because there is no other visible course for them to follow if they are to make their way in world markets.

## FROM KOJÈVE TO FUKUYAMA

Reflecting on the opportunities, or lack of them, that face Eastern Europeans today, one could conclude, upon reading Hegel's *Phenomenology of Spirit*, that they have reached the end of history. In a remarkable turnabout in recent thought, it is neo-liberal economists who now entertain this possibility. The phrase 'the end of history', which has been brooded on by European students of Hegel since the early nineteenth century, has been brought to the attention of a wider readership by Fukuyama. In his article, he observed that:

'In watching the flow of events over the past decade or so, it is hard to avoid the feeling that something very fundamental has happened in world history . . . the century that began full of self-confidence in the ultimate triumph of Western liberal democracy seems at its close to be returning full circle to where it started: not to an "end of ideology" or a convergence between capitalism and socialism, as earlier predicted, but to an unabashed victory of economic and political liberalism.'[4]

By stating it in this manner, Fukuyama helped to give a widely held view a sharper edge. Had he stopped there, he would have been echoing a commonplace about the ending of the Cold War. But he went further, and by doing so he provoked often abusive rebuttal from uncomprehending critics:

> 'The Triumph of the West, of the Western *idea*, is evident first of all in the total exhaustion of viable systematic alternatives to Western liberalism . . . What we may be witnessing is not just the end of the Cold War, or the passing of a particular period of post-war history, but the end of history as such: that is, the end point of mankind's evolution and the universalisation of Western liberal democracy as the final form of human government.'[5]

In his advocacy of the 'end of history', Fukuyama is, of course, reaching back to Kojève and to Hegel. Because Fukuyama's use of the term 'the end of history' has been perversely misunderstood, his own words on the issue deserve careful reading, especially by the school of 'commonsense' commentators:

> 'Kojève sought to resurrect the Hegel of the *Phenomenology of Spirit*, the Hegel who proclaimed history to be at an end in 1806. For as early as this Hegel saw in Napoleon's defeat of the Prussian monarchy at the Battle of Jena the victory of the ideals of the French Revolution, and the imminent universalisation of the state incorporating the principles of liberty and equality . . . To say that history ended in 1806 meant that mankind's ideological evolution ended in the ideals of the French and American Revolutions; while particular regimes in the real world might not implement these ideals fully, their theoretical truth is absolute and could not be improved upon . . . We might summarise the content of the universal homogenous state as liberal democracy in the political sphere combined with easy access to VCRs and stereos in the economic.'[6]

This suggests that Hegel, whatever his early nineteenth century blinkers, has not only proved to be a seminal generator of provocative and stylish texts, but is also a bookish 'real presence' of some intellectual weight in the contemporary discussion of world affairs. It will be argued here that the status of Hegelian thought as 'a past that is a present' (to borrow a phrase from Hegel's great critic, Kierkegaard) extends to the claim that Hegel may also prove to be something of an honorary Orientalist.

A beginning can be made by noting what has been artfully elided in Fukuyama's neo-liberal reading of Kojève. First, there is the uncomfortable, if understandable, way he imposes a near-uniformity of meaning and ideological character on the French and American Revolutions. It is obvious, or should be, that when the 'Petition of the Agitators to the Legislative Assembly' on 20 June 1792 proclaimed that 'The image of the *Patrie* is the sole divinity which it is permissible to worship', the French Revolution broke with both American and East European sensibility. Abbé Sieyès insisted in 'What is the Third Estate?' (1789) that 'The nation exists before all, it is the origin of everything. Its will is always legal, it is the law itself.' He veered sharply away from the weak theory of state and nation, which has characterised almost all Anglo-American political reflection since Locke, towards traditional Continental theory.

Whatever the personal shock of Hegel's encounter with history at the Battle of Jena – he was a witness to Napoleon's victorious campaign – the German philosopher was, in his youth, a student of the Scottish Enlightenment, and recognised early the epochal importance of Locke's revolutionary doctrine and of England's industrial revolution. Nevertheless, to concede the importance of something is not necessarily to embrace it. In a way not true of either Kojève or Hegel, Fukuyama's celebration of the American way of life, his recipe of 'economic and political liberalism', smells more like *réchauffé* Manchester School economics than the Hegel of even Georg Lukács' Marxist, therefore economic-minded, biography.

There is a further twist in Fukuyama's borrowing of the notion of an 'end of history'. Hegel's strict concept of 'absolute knowledge' has had little impact on public philosophic discourse in the English-speaking world, but the conviction of finality that Fukuyama, and most neo-liberals, ascribe to the doctrine of free markets can be seen to embody a conviction-politics version of absolute knowledge, although one finally more political than philosophical in content. Hegel would not have approved. This may say something damning about the nature of the debate over how best to revitalise the economies of Eastern Europe. All too often neo-conservative wisdom has painted in absolutist tones.

The Japanese model, as imitated across the face of East and South East Asia, suggests that Fukuyama is wrong. There may be another path for a nation to take, and one that is more consistent with European identity and history, and its ontology, its mediated sense of self.[8]

One lacuna of Fukuyama's definition of Hegel's 'universal state' as political liberalism plus 'easy access to VCRs and stereos' hints at a vulnerability in his reasoning. Fukuyama unctuously refers to 'access to', not to the manufacture of, VCRs and stereos. In the wake of the collapse of America's domestic electronics industry before the advance of East Asian and even West European competition, what else could he say? Such contentious issues point to the larger question of whether the American way of life does provide the sole comprehensive definition of the universe of the future. They underscore the significance of the Japanese model and raise questions about the wisdom of the campaign to persuade Eastern Europeans to embrace a monetarist-driven revolution.

## JAPAN AND HEGEL

Drawing on Hegel's political philosophy, a different picture of Eastern Europe's predicament can be drawn. In his *Philosophy of Right*, he defines civil society as the community of producers and consumers. He sees civil society as but a single, if crucial, dimension of society as a whole, which also includes the state, the family and related kinship groupings. In the most radical of monetarist readings, on the other hand, the sole obligation and duty of the present states in Eastern Europe is for them to fall on their swords. This may be perfectly consistent with non-liberal ideology, but such a hope is incompatible with European political tradition or the likely future of the eastern half of the continent.

Hegel's approach to thinking about civil society allows us to 'bracket' (in Husserl's sense) some of the more dogmatic or foundational assumptions (*die Grundprobleme*) of neo-conservative proponents of Hegelian doctrine, such as Fukuyama's. Hegel's vision encourages us to see that civil societies are made, not born: made, in some cases, by the state. It can be insisted that all late capitalist states, from nineteenth-century Germany and Japan to contemporary Poland and Korea (the South today, the North tomorrow) have been obliged to fashion, animate, and direct their own versions of 'civil society'. This contradicts the economic liberalism that has been urged on Central and East European societies. This contradiction does not apply to the Japanese 'development state' model. The Meiji state first created itself from the ruins of the Tokugawa regime, and then tried to discipline and direct Japan's answer to 'civil society', an approach much closer to Hegel's idea than, for example, to Locke's in *An Essay Concerning the True Original, Extent, and End of Civil Government* (1690) or Adam Ferguson's in *An Essay on the History of Civil Society* (1767).

True, the idea of 'civil society' translates only poorly into the Japanese language. The expression '*shimin-shakai*' has little meaning for the Japanese. In fact, it is sometimes difficult to distinguish precisely between the terms 'state' and 'nation' in the Japanese language. Just what did Prime Minister Nakasone Yasuhiro mean when he insisted that Japan must become a *kokusai-kokka*? 'An international state or nation', is the most prosaic of renderings, 'A nation among nations' comes closer.

Such Japanese incomprehension of Eastern European concepts has another dimension. Consider, for example, the sustained effort of the Bush administration to liberalise Japan's markets. This acrimonious American campaign may be seen as an attempt to strengthen the foundations of Japan's civil society. But how is it possible, at this late stage of Japan's economic ascent, that American policymakers are still trying to turn Japan into the kind of civil society that would win the approval of Smith or Hume or Bentham? This interminable American crusade to reshape the essence of the Japanese polity must thus far be judged to have failed. Post-war Germany has also become a capitalist democracy in its own way. The examples of Japan or Germany suggest that a fundamental pluralism may be at work in the world's encounter with modernity. Eastern European reformers should not ignore such pluralism.

YELLOW ATHENA

The Japanese achievement should not be seen as an inevitable consequence of human nature, as eighteenth-century empiricists interpreted this term, or philosophical essence or scientific monism, but rather as the product of pragmatic thought and experiment, invigorated by the force of political imagination and theory. Just as a great novelist, such as Proust, may literally extend the reach of our sensibility, the Japanese experience should enlarge the Western sense of the possible in any definition of dynamic social order and human governance. Perhaps it takes an Hegelian like Kojève to see that Japan's heroic drive to modernise is part of an extraordinary *intellectual* conquest. Whatever Japan's failings, and they are many, it is the achievement of mind that makes the teachings and philosophical foundations of her miracle into Japan's supreme gift to contemporary European thought. It can be seen to make post-war Japan into a 'yellow Athena'.

Japan's post-war miracle, as a model of competitive success, confirms the *'pluralité des mondes'* (to adopt Fontenelle's phrase) of the social world of man. The Japanese model illuminates, with unique force, the idea of 'pluralism' as it is used, for example, by Sir Isaiah Berlin in his essay 'The Pursuit of the Ideal'.[9] At work in monetarist economics, as in all positive economic theory, is a kind of dogmatic monism. This is Berlin's summary of this tendency:

'At some point I realised that what all these views [of the eighteenth-century empiricists and their predecessors] had in common was a Platonic ideal: in the first place that, as in the sciences, all genuine questions must have one true answer and one only, all the rest being necessarily errors; in the second place, that there must be a dependable path towards the discovery of such truths; in the third place, that the true answers, when found, must necessarily be compatible with one another and form a single whole, for one truth cannot be incompatible with another – that we knew *a priori*.'[10]

Later, upon reading Machiavelli, Vico and Herder, Berlin confesses the need he felt to revise this view. The discovery of the true meaning of pluralism, he admits, came as a shock, but it encouraged him to rethink the conventional definition of political pluralism:

' "I prefer coffee, you prefer champagne. We have different tastes. There is no more to be said." That is relativism. But Herder's view, and Vico's, is not that: it is what I should describe as pluralism – that is, the conception that there are many different ends that men may seek and still be fully rational, fully men, fully capable of understanding each other, as we derive it from reading Plato or the novels of medieval Japan – worlds, outlooks, very remote from our own.'[11]

In their rational pursuit of ends that differ from those posited by the Anglo-American economic model, the modern Japanese have demonstrated, with unique force the importance of Berlin's doctrine of pluralism. Thus defined, pluralism should encourage us to resist economic Procrusteanism both when interpreting Japan and applying the lessons of its experience elsewhere. The Japanese experience is theirs; the lessons are ours to draw.

In *Black Athena: The Afroasiatic Roots of Classical Civilization*, Martin Bernal has argued that the classic Greeks were 'black' in a flat racial sense and that the chief intellectual fruits that have traditionally been viewed as the products of European Greece were in fact derived from the Levant and ancient Egypt.[12] The racial matrix of thought may be of interest, but thought is vastly more important than race. To describe Japan as a 'yellow Athena' is to reject Bernal's racist approach.

In Hegel's essay on tragedy as dramatic art, he used Athena, the goddess, to stand for the life of classical Athens, imagined in its essential unity. To call Japan a 'yellow Athena' is to raise three issues. First, it is to stress that, in a way analogous to the modern Japanese polity, the ancient Greeks rarely drew the distinction between public and private spheres, and when they did primacy was constantly accorded to what the modern European would call the public sphere. The ancient Greeks were not individualistic in the modern European sense; they lacked what Hegel called the subjective moral sense. It is important to recall that *civilis societas* is a Latin doctrine; not a Greek one.

In this attitude to society, if in no other, Japanese tradition stands closer to that of classical Athens. Hegel saw the modern subjective moral sense as setting post-Renaissance Europeans above the ancient Greeks, but it is this emphasis on an inner moral sense, articulated by Kant, that contributes to the unrealism of modern moralistic doctrines, such as Rawls' *A Theory of Justice*. The Japanese example should encourage us to assay the impact of such moral doctrines on the West's economic life.

Secondly, modern Japanese practice may be seen also to concur with the Continental statist interpretation of Socrates' final gesture of submission not only to the lay, but to the *polis*, to the state. The doctrine is set out in the *Crito*; the gesture in the *Apology*. Thirdly, to treat Japan as a 'yellow Athena' is an attempt to domesticate an alien political tradition to Western circumstance, to make reflection on this Oriental polity into a cardinal intellectual move *within* our tradition. This is something the West has not attempted since medieval times and not even contemplated in over three centuries. To give such concerns a skin-deep gloss is also to acknowledge the racial hurt that stands behind the bitter anti-Europeanism of nationalist intellectuals, including *Nihonjin-ron-sha*.

To plead for a 'yellow Athena' is to urge the recognition that, after more than 25 centuries, the Western dialogue on the nature of government and the meaning of politics should embrace a continuum that will reach from ancient Athens to modern Japan. A reading of the Japanese model should shake us, as Berlin's encounter with Machiavelli shook him.

Such an encounter has methodological implications for the Western, or – if American scholars are uncomfortable, under the pressure of 'political correctness', with the term 'Western' – the European, political theorist. The present predicament of the post-communist countries of Europe points to the need to develop a political version of *la nouvelle critique*, one that is concerned with the applications of the lessons and language of classic political texts *to the present*. This approach will stand opposed to *la critique universitaire*, again to borrow from the debate in French literary circles over classic texts in the 1960s, which for academic reasons defines the job of the textual interpretation in narrower, period-bound terms, a method dominated by textual positivism. Applying Hegelian thought to the present demands a fresh approach.

## CIVIL SOCIETY IN HEGELIAN PERSPECTIVE

In the 'Theory' section of List's *The National System of Political Economy*, he analyses some of the implications of classical political economy. He takes issue with the claim of economists in the Smithian tradition to have evolved a universal science; that political economy, in the words of J.B. Say, 'lastly, relates to the interests of all nations, to human society in general'.[13]

Again, the issue here turns on a defence of pluralism. In pursuing the worthy goal of a universal science, classical political economists, in List's view, willfully neglect the importance of the nation in the name of the profit-maximising individual. The root of the limitation may be traced to the ontology of classical political economists which acknowledges the existence only of individuals: the nation is, as it were, a fiction. As List notes, 'The first of the North American advocates of free trade, as understood by Adam Smith – Thomas Cooper, President of Columbia College – denies even the existence of nationality; he calls the nation "a grammatical invention", created only to save periphrases, a nonentity, which has no actual existence save in the heads of politicians'.[14] And, one might add, in the heads of the peoples of East Asia and Eastern Europe.

Margaret Thatcher's attack on the idea of 'society', her insistence that only individuals exist, not collectivities, may be seen to repeat the same error. But Mrs Thatcher's argument is part of a long tradition among English-speaking theorists. The main intellectual consequence of such methodological individualism, the philosophical conceit that only individuals exist, is that in nearly every Anglo-American meditation on the nature of civil society, the state, like Lewis Carroll's Cheshire Cat, is at best a spectral presence, and all too often disappears.

The anti-statist propensity within Anglo-American reasoning has often aroused considerable suspicion among those educated outside this tradition. The counter-orthodoxy, Continental-European or East-Asian, has proven unbearable to English-speaking neo-liberals. Indeed this ideological intolerance may be seen to have fomented a kind of conceptual imperialism in recent English-language thinking on the 'problematic' (as the term is used by Althusser) posed by the relationship of state and market.

Thus in the name of the Anglo-Saxon ontology (the rationally disciplined self-understanding of a society) not only is the East European or Japanese Ontology (its meditated sense of collective identity) willfully misunderstood, but its right to continued existence is denied. The claims of a European or Japanese ontology to validity are dismissed in the name of universal science. The final cut is contained in the discovery that this universal science is in practice, if not in theory, the congealed essence of English or American commonsense. In other words, Eastern Europe and Japan are to be redesigned to suit the insights and the whims of what is nothing more than the ruling ontology of

American and British society.

## THE LIMITS OF ENGLISH THOUGHT

The problem is well illustrated in one of the most generous and open-minded readings of Hegel's *Philosophy of Right* in the English language: John Plamenatz's treatment of Hegel's theory of civil society in his two-volume study, *Man and Society*.[15] According to Plamenatz, 'civil society' as Hegel conceives of it, may be roughly defined as 'a community of producers of the kind described by the classical economists together with the public services needed to maintain order inside it.'[16] This definition is similar to the Victorian notion of the 'night-watchman state'. This also highlights the shift of interest in English-language theorising from 'producers' to 'consumers'.

But Hegel insists that society is more than just a collection of individuals, more than just civil society. It includes, notably, both the family and the state. Plamenatz concedes:

'If Hegel had studied Hume's or Bentham's theory of the State, he would doubtless have said that it falls far short of the truth, taking no account of what the State essentially is. What Bentham or Hume called the State would have seemed to him merely an aspect of civil society.'[17]

If civil society is, in Plamenatz's reformulated definition, merely 'the whole system of economic and political relations considered as satisfying individual needs and serving private ends' alone, then Hegel would reject such a notion as providing an inadequate concept of the state, the nation, the family or society as a whole.[18]

Beyond this Plamenatz will not go. Like Moses, he is allowed to see the conceptual promised land, but is not permitted to enter it because of the intellectual tradition with which he identifies and which he thinks is valid. Hegel did not suffer from this limitation:

'The State is actual only when its members have a feeling of their own self-hood, and it is stable only when public and private ends are identical.'[19]

The most important part of Hegel's observation is the first four words: 'The State is actual'. This Plamenatz, despite his open-mindedness, cannot accept. It is not therefore only Hume and Bentham who can be seen to have 'an inadequate theory of the State', but Plamenatz himself. He comes very close to the boundary of disciplined English-language understanding of the state when he draws this line on his Hegelian peregrinations, a line he will not cross. If Plamenatz cannot cross it, even as a thought-experiment, then what monetarist would even attempt to transgress it. What else are we to make of the ontological timidity of his observation that:

'Society or the community or the State, except where we use these words elliptically to mean those who govern or exert the greatest influence on others is not active; it is merely a sphere of activity, a living concept of men.'[20]

'The State is not actual.' Is there a nineteenth-century or twentieth-century European nationalist or post-war East Asian state-builder who would accept this view? The political philosophy reflected in the Japanese model rejects this position out of hand. The argument can be put more strongly. If, for example, MITI officials *think* the Anglo-American view of the state is untrue, *act* as if this view were untrue, and *achieve* results which demonstrate that this view is untrue, then at some point neo-liberal political philosophers will need to rethink their position. In the meantime, it is not obvious that East European thinkers and politicians should be made to jump hoops to suit the expectations of their monetarist critics. It is conceivable that Hegel was right, and that history did end at Jena in 1806. Fukuyama would wrap the triumphs of Americanism in 1945 and 1989 in this Hegelian cloak. But Kojève points to a different contest, and it is not obvious that the 'yellow Athena' has lost it.

## NOTES

1. Francis Fukuyama, 'The End of History', *The National Interest*, Summer 1989 issue, pp. 3–18.
2. *Hegel's Philosophy of Right*, translated by T.M. Knox, Oxford, Clarendon Press, 1952.
3. Alexandre Kojève, *Introduction to the Reading of Hegel: Lectures on the Phenomenology of Spirit*, assembled by Raymond Queneau, edited by Allan Bloom, translated by James H. Nichols, Jr, Ithaca and London, Cornell University Press, 1989. Footnote of pp. 161–2
4. Fukuyama, *op.cit.*, p. 3.
5. *Ibid.*, pp. 3–4.

6. *Ibid.*, pp. 4–5 and p. 8.
7. Georg Lukács, *The Young Hegel: Studies in the Relations between Dialectics and Economics*, translated by Rodney Livingstone, London, Merlin Press, 1975.
8. The notion of 'ontology/Ontology' will be developed in a forthcoming study by David Williams.
9. Isaiah Berlin, *The Crooked Timber of Humanity: Chapters in the History of Ideas*, London, John Murray, 1990, pp. 1–19.
10. *Ibid.*, pp. 5–6.
11. *Ibid.*, p. 11.
12. Martin Bernal, *Black Athena: The Afroasiatic Roots of Classical Civilization, Vol I: The Fabrication of Ancient Greece 1785–1985*, London Free Association Books, 1987.
13. Friedrich List, *The National System of Political Economy*, translated by Sampson S. Lloyd, London, Longmans, Green and Co., 1922, p. 98.
14. *Ibid.*, p. 99.
15. John Plamenatz, *Man and Society: A Critical Examination of Some Important Social and Political Theories from Machiavelli to Marx*, London, Longman, 1963.
16. *Ibid.*, Vol. II, pp. 232–3.
17. *Ibid.*, Vol. II, p. 245.
18. *Ibid.*, Vol. II, pp. 245–6.
19. Hegel, *op.cit.* Addition 158 to par. 265, p. 281.
20. Plamenatz, *op.cit.*, p. 242.

# Index

175

Printed in the United Kingdom
by Lightning Source UK Ltd.
105322UKS00001B/192